MUSIC FOI

MUSIC FOR
G.C.E. 'O' LEVEL

JANE CORBETT
A.R.C.M.

VERA YELVERTON
A.R.C.M.

BARRIE & JENKINS
COMMUNICA - EUROPA

© 1961 by Jane Corbett and Vera Yelverton
First published 1961 by
Barrie and Rockliff (Barrie Books Ltd.)
2 Clement's Inn, Strand, London WC2
Printed in Great Britain
at the Alden Press, Oxford
Second Edition 1967

Second Edition, revised 1973
Reprinted 1975
Reprinted 1978 by Barrie and Jenkins
24 Highbury Crescent
London N5 1RX

ISBN 0 214 165761

CONTENTS

Preface

FOR SOME CONSIDERABLE TIME the need has been felt for a comprehensive book which will take the student to the General Certificate of Education in Music, Ordinary Level. In the following pages an attempt has been made to put theoretical points in a clear and historical way, aiming to unite theory with practice at every level of study.

The chapter on aural training and sight-reading is the reflection of modern ideas, whereby it is not taken for granted that every student knows how to sing or play the examples given, and in which guidance is offered on this most basic and important branch of musical knowledge.

Some musical terms, ornaments and meanings have altered during many years of use and are no longer at all precise—for example, the terms 'concord' and 'discord'. A reorganization seems overdue, especially for the purpose of examination standards.

The student who may find this book most useful is likely to be between the ages of eleven and sixteen, and this has been borne in mind by the authors.

Although the different syllabuses vary in detail, the main requirements for G.C.E. Music, O. Level, are:

Paper I. Aural tests.

Paper II. Theory and harmony.

Papers III and IV. History of music, form, knowledge of orchestral and keyboard instruments and the orchestral score, detailed knowledge of a prescribed composition and of a prescribed composer and his works.

Exemption from a part of some of the following syllabuses:

1. Cambridge Local Examinations Syndicate, Cambridge;
2. Oxford Local Examinations Delegacy, Oxford;
3. Oxford and Cambridge Schools Examination Board, 74 High Street, Oxford;
4. University Entrance and School Examinations Council, University of London, Senate House, W.C.1;
5. Durham University School Examinations Board, 6 Eldon Place, Newcastle-upon-Tyne, 2;

is allowed to candidates who have recently been successful in passing a Grade V or VI practical examination of the Associated Board, and/or Grade V Theory papers. Details can be obtained from the addresses above, and also specimen examination papers.

For advanced students the purchase of selected books mentioned in the Bibliography is desirable, but, as this is naturally an expensive undertaking, they may be borrowed from school or public libraries.

It is felt by the authors that the chapters in this book should be studied before reading the recommended books in order to memorize the salient points of each facet of musical knowledge, as these books will naturally contain much more detailed information.

Acquisition of musical knowledge and practice is nowadays considered more and more as a 'discipline'. Universities and schools are increasingly inclined to give music a place in their syllabuses, as it trains eye, hand and memory, besides providing relaxation from other studies and pursuits. Public performance and the arranging of concerts and operas provide the young student with experience of situations demanding self-control, planning and co-operative effort in order to win the appreciation of an audience. Such experience is valuable for any person wishing to embark on a career involving administrative or public work.

Acknowledgments

THE AUTHORS WOULD LIKE to tender their thanks to Mr. Geoffrey Corbett, Opera and Ballet Conductor, at present Musical Director of London's Festival Ballet, for his contribution of the chapter on the orchestra and orchestral score; Mr. Norman Anderson, Professor and Examiner at the Guildhall School of Music and Drama, for his advice on Musical Ornaments and the Piano; Iréne Armitage, B.Mus., A.R.C.M., teacher of Harmony and Composition at Hendon Technical College, for checking the chapters on Form and Harmony; Elizabeth Evans, L.R.A.M., A.R.C.M., G.R.S.M., and Betty Vowles, L.R.A.M., for helpful notes on the chapters on Scales and Aural Work; Mr. Hughes, of Herrburger Brooks, for permission to print the Schwander Action diagram in the chapter on Keyboard Instruments; Mr. Squibb, of Steinway & Son, for useful notes on the working of Steinway Pianos; and Miss Jillian Perry, who having recently passed her G.C.E. in music, gave invaluable advice and information from an examinee's angle.

CHAPTER ONE

The History of Music

'MUSIC IS A SACRED ART.' Throughout the history of the world, since the first creatures had ears to hear, sound has conveyed emotion,—warning, love and sorrow, joy and fear. Primeval man had much in nature to teach him melody—the songs of birds, the sounds of brooks and waterfalls, the sighing of the wind through reeds, the cries of animals. Very early in man's history music became an emotional release in which primitive people expressed feelings with the beating of drums and tribal dances, wailing wild chants in an ever-rising tempo of excitement. Instruments of plucked strings and reed pipes came into use all over the ancient world. The dithyramb, a religious hymn during the performance of which priestesses and people alike reached feverish heights of ecstasy culminating in human sacrifice and orgies, led to the Greek drama, in which the chorus played an important part.

In the Eastern world religious songs and dances have developed in many and varied forms, and their music with its quarter tones has strange inflexions to our ears. Despite apparent differences, a link may exist between the modes used in Eastern and Western melodies or they may have developed independently.

But perhaps the swiftest development came in Europe. After the fall of the Roman Empire and during the Dark Ages, all culture was kept alive by the monasteries of the Church of Rome. As more and more peoples of the conquering barbarians were won to Christianity, so were more and more efforts made to stamp out the existing songs and folk-melodies associated with paganism and witchcraft. Women were forbidden to officiate in the churches and church music itself had to follow very rigid rules. Plainsong, derived from what were mistakenly thought to be Greek modes and from some aspects of Jewish religious music, became established in the church.

Continuity of lay music was sustained by the epic bard and the minstrel. The troubadour played and sang his part in the courts of kings in the twelfth and thirteenth centuries. 'Sumer Is Icumen In' was written by a monk in the thirteenth century and at the same time has a contrapuntal complexity belonging to the fifteenth.

As the courts of kings increased in importance, so music became more in demand to charm and amuse the great between their wars and skirmishes. With the rise of commerce and trade and the discovery of new lands, great wealth was accrued and settled courts gave rise to the appointment of men of talent and genius who could provide great music to divert and please. In sixteenth- and seventeenth-century England William Byrd, Purcell and Handel wrote for kings and Church and in France Lully, Rameau and Couperin, together with countless others, produced music with all the formality and flourish relished by the French Court. In Italy Palestrina brought contrapuntal music to greater heights, and the male castrati of these two centuries and the one which followed developed Italian song to beauties which perhaps have never since been recaptured. Italian opera came into being during this time, helped forward by the greatness of Monteverdi in the first half of the seventeenth century.

In Germany, European music reached its greatest peak. The small princely courts or electorates survived later than in most other European countries, and each court had its appointed musicians, well paid to supply music for church and festival. With so many places to be filled, music became a desired profession and a tradition amongst musical families. Johann Sebastian Bach came from a large family of musicians, and many of them had appointments in various towns all over Germany, meeting once a year for a family reunion. The sanity and settled peace of this is reflected in the gloriously developed contrapuntal style of Bach and the greatness and sanctity of his music written for the Lutheran Church. In keeping abreast of the new developments in instrument building, Bach employed the new well-tempered klavier, for which he wrote his *Forty-eight Preludes and Fugues* in all keys, this being possible for the first time.

The German and Austrian tradition of every town of note supporting its own musical life gave the background for the flowering of a rich musical culture.

Mozart, unique as a child genius, travelled to many of the courts of Europe, performing with his gifted sister and under the guidance of his father, a violinist. The boy was knighted by the Pope when only fourteen. Mozart composed sonatas, symphonies and even operas before his teens, and his work, based on old forms, contained much of German and Austrian folk-song idiom as well as the Italian song style over a plucked string accompaniment. In his mature work, as in the work of his older friend Haydn, Mozart increases the scope of sonata-form in his solo sonatas, chamber works and symphonies. However, the interest of princes was not great enough to keep him from poverty, despair in his private life and early death, followed by burial in a pauper's grave.

Beethoven, also from a musical family, was trained with the whip in early life to a high standard of musical knowledge and performance, made a further break with formalism to express the new freedom of the individual. He made more extensive use of key changes and modulations and, through the medium of the piano, small ensembles, the orchestra and choirs, produced expressions of human, philosophical and abstract thought which, perhaps, have never been surpassed.

Then came Schubert, who, besides writing a great deal of orchestral, chamber and piano music, wrote hundreds of songs and began the great tradition of German *Lieder*. He was followed by Schumann and Mendelssohn, who gave expression to the new romanticism, as well as Chopin and Liszt, who revolutionized piano technique; this being possible because of improvements in the instrument. Chopin, the very embodiment of a genius of the Romantic Age, became acknowledged as one of the greatest musical miniaturists of the piano and a considerable harmonic innovator, while Liszt, the star pianist of his day, developed an approach to the use of thematic material which powerfully influenced the works of his son-in-law, Richard Wagner.

In France the rise of the middle classes created the demand for larger concert halls and bigger orchestras. Berlioz responded to this demand by composing for an orchestra which he enlarged even further than Beethoven, who might be thought of as the man who established the composition of the modern symphony orchestra. Wagner, through the medium of German opera, utilized this enlarged orchestra for the production of mammoth works of new revolutionary nature. He saw opera as a unification and expression of all the arts (*gesamkunstwerk*) and his opera music develops symphonically as a whole by means of recurring themes (*lietmotiven*) and thematic transformation. He broke away from the old forms of recitative and aria.

On the other hand, Brahms, his inspiration rooted in the classical tradition, continued to explore the symphony and sonata and, at the same time, writing some beautiful Romantic songs.

Whilst Germany struggled for unity and dominance in the military field, she, together with Austria, continued to give the conditions for musical expression of the deepest kind. Bruckner within himself showed the most astounding compounds of romanticism, catholicism and modernity. Mahler, Jewish and Viennese, put into musical language the whole flowering culture and decay of the *Fin de Siécle* or end of the century—in fact, the end of an epoch, as it later proved to be. Perhaps a whole decade of enchanting decadence is expressed in his symphony, *Das Lied von der Erde* (The Song of the Earth). Richard Strauss carried romanticism into the modern era, largely through the medium of opera and tone poem, and Schoenberg startled a generation with his atonal music founded on a twelve-note system of tone rows and influencing a large proportion of twentieth-century musicians.

Music in other countries had also developed greatly. In Italy the tradition for song and opera was carried forward by the work of such dramatic geniuses as Rossini, Verdi and Puccini.

In Czechoslovakia, Smetana founded a national school which Dvořák brought to its peak, Janaček was its greatest modern exponent. Grieg epitomized the northern romanticism of Norway, and Glinka, Rimsky-Korsakov, Tchaikovsky, Mussorgsky and others acquainted the world with Russian national music.

In France, the opera of Bizet and César Franck's symphonic form moulded French music into a style more Latin than German. At the turn of the century Debussy reflected French impressionism in operatic, orchestral and piano music, effecting as much advance in piano technique and composition in his own day as Liszt and Chopin in theirs. The national taste for impressionism and small-scale music has been carried forward into the twentieth century by Ravel, Poulenc and others, who also portray the realist and Catholic thought of France today.

Bartók, teacher, pianist and composer, brought Hungarian rhythms to new life, and his piano music, chromatic and percussive, introduced fresh modes of performance to the instrument. Bartók emigrated to America and took American nationality, as did the Russian composer and pianist, Rachmaninoff, whose decadent romanticism was conveyed in the glittering brilliance of his performances and compositions, and Stravinsky, whose ballet music, symphonic and choral music has created new worlds for the listener.

In Germany, traditional influences evolved into a neo-classicist school, with Hindemith as its leading exponent. Sibelius in Finland conveyed the national pride of his country to an admiring world, and Spanish music, through de Falla and others, has kept its own particular flavour of flamenco and guitar-playing.

In England, a great revival of music has occurred in the last fifty years. This revival, begun by Parry and Stanford, was carried forward by Elgar and Delius, resulting in a strongly nationalistic school in which such composers as Vaughan Williams, Arthur Bliss, Arnold Bax, John Ireland and Benjamin Britten have brought English music to a very high level.

In Russia, Prokofieff and Shostakovitch, amongst many others, have evolved new patterns and styles, essentially Russian in character, but embodying twentieth-century realism. Government requests to write music which ordinary people can understand have resulted in the composition of music of greater tonality, strangely bringing Russian music nearer to that of the Western world, where many serious composers write for stage and screen, owing to the fact that the demand for music in these media is greater than that of the concert platform. This music has to be of a quality which the mass of the people can understand and enjoy, and therefore, in the West, jazz and folk-music are the bases for much new music which has been produced. In America, Gershwin and Leonard Bernstein have been exponents of this kind of music, and such leading figures as Samuel Barber and Aaron Copland employ much American folk-music as their thematic material.

This short chapter on the growth of music in Europe has made very little mention of the performer, through whom the thoughts of the composer are conveyed to the listener—the opera star, the virtuoso conductor, the instrumentalist, whose art has been moulded over the centuries and whose skill acquired with much pain and effort by the individual. Neither has anything been stated regarding the instrument-builders, such as the great Stradivari, violin-maker of the seventeenth century, the inventors of the harpsichord and the modern piano, the musicologists, the builders of concert halls, the impresarios and the teachers of music. Very many important composers, such as Gluck, have been omitted altogether, and the student is urged to read as much as possible regarding them and to refer to the Chronology of this book, and to the chapters on harmony and form.

CHAPTER TWO

Time and Rhythm

AT THE VERY COMMENCEMENT of musical study the student should be quite clear as to the differing meanings of RHYTHM and TIME.

From man's primitive beginnings RHYTHM, as a steady, basic beat or pulse, has had a very special significance. The chanting of primitive tribes was accompanied by drum-beats in peculiar rhythms, reinforced by the stamping of dancers' feet. Very early in history it was found that labour was carried out more easily by bands of people singing and working in rhythm. Sea shanties and work songs are only a continuation of this custom.

But whilst rhythm is the basic pulse of music and poetic speech, it was found that this was subdivided into different sections of TIME; hence the Greek method of dividing hexameters into feet or metres and accents, such as the kind taken over by the English-speaking poets, e.g.:

'The | *dusk*-y | *night* rides | *down* the | *sky*'

from which it can be seen that the accent falls rhythmically, such as it might do in the barring of music.

When medieval men felt the need for writing down music instead of handing down church songs (plainsong) and lay songs (folk-songs) from generation to generation by the simple means of singing them, they firstly made use of the system of the Roman Boethius (A.D. 470-525), which comprised giving the notes of the two octaves, then in use, the first fifteen letters of the alphabet.

Later on other methods were tried, but by the ninth and tenth centuries whilst the letters A-G were retained for note-naming, proportional TIME notation was introduced on a stave of first one and then four lines, in a specific shape:

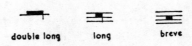

double long   long   breve

each of which were theoretically worth a half or third of the time of the preceding one.

After many experiments, the notation and time values we use today were evolved. The breve, ‖○‖, (rest ⊨⊓), is the longest note, though rarely used today, and is twice the length of the semibreve ○ or whole note.

The notes which are in use now and their equivalent rests or periods of silence are tabled as follows:

SEMIBREVE ○ Rest ▬ Hanging down from second line of five-lined stave

= 2 MINIMS ♩ ♩ Rest ▬ Resting on third line of stave

= 4 CROTCHETS ♩ ♩ ♩ ♩ Rest ⸙ or ⸖

= 8 QUAVERS ♫ ♫ ♪ ♪ ♪ ♪ Rest ⸲

=16 SEMIQUAVERS ♬♬♬♬ ♬♬♬♬♬ ♬ ♬ ♬ ♬ Rest ⸳

=32 DEMISEMIQUAVERS ♬ ♬♬♬♬ Rest ⸴

=64 HEMIDEMISEMIQUAVERS ♬ ♬♬♬♬ Rest ⸵

from which it will be seen that the principle of each note having a time value of half the previous one is now very strictly adhered to. If a note is required which has a slightly different value, this can be indicated by writing a dot beside the note, which makes it worth its own value plus half as much again, e.g. ♩· = ♩ ♩ ♩. Leopold Mozart, father of the famous Wolfgang Amadeus Mozart, invented the double dot, which makes the note worth not only half as much again, but half that half again as well, e.g. ♩·· = ♩ ♩ ♩ ♪.

Bar lines ▤▤▤ gradually came into use in the fifteenth and sixteenth centuries, although at first they were only inserted here and there in scores of concerted music as an aid to the eye. Bar lines have usually been added by editors to music of this period and may be much at fault.

Time signatures were evolved as used today and are set out in the following table:

Many composers of today use other and more complex time signatures, such as $\frac{5}{4}$ ♩♩♩♩♩ and $\frac{7}{4}$ ♩♩♩♩♩♩♩. This is often in an effort to obtain freer forms or to resurrect the old type of unbarred music.

Other irregular times can be notated by the use of the tie (see Chapter on Musical Signs) or written out as follows:

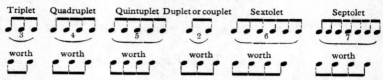

These have to be played in the same time as would be taken up by the notes which they are worth, and often prove difficult of achievement by pianists. See the above examples and, for instance, Excursion No. 3 from *Excursions for the Piano*, by Samuel Barber.

CHAPTER THREE

Scales and Their Key Signatures

IN ALL ARTS AND CRAFTS the means to express the individual, or communal, idea is governed by the available techniques. These techniques in turn are limited by the tools which have been devised by man to produce the results his imagination can foresee.

Human foresight, based on past experience, leaps ahead of the current tools, demanding something additional, or different, to fashion a fresh aspect. In the practice of music the various instruments which produce sound have changed many times in detail in order to express more subtle ideas.

For the composer the invention of scales gave him one of his most useful tools.

Some of the ancient civilizations of the world, among them Persian, Chinese and Greek, had a written notation based partly on the range of human voices and partly on their instruments, which indicated scale plans. In time the church musicians of the Western world emerged as the most lucid organizers of scales, although of a kind not much in use now, but on which the modern forms as we know them are based. Their scales were called 'modes', and each had a different order of tones and semitones, approximating to the white notes of the piano, but they were intended mainly as a guide for melodic writing. *See page 29*

From about the ninth century, through years of gradual change, in which the expansion of schemes of notation was extremely important, the major, harmonic and melodic minor and the chromatic scales were evolved as the best framework for melody and harmony. By the seventeenth and eighteenth centuries these scales were orthodox for all European compositions and remained so until, in their turn, they have become something of a limitation, hindering the way to further progress.

Most present-day composers still base their work consciously or unconsciously on these scales, but some are using new methods of combining hitherto irreconcilable sounds, rhythmic freedoms and experimental qualities of tone, bewildering in their diversity, all of which reveal dissatisfaction with what are considered old-fashioned tools. All these tendencies are of immense interest to students of music and should be followed sympathetically as the inevitable process of human imagination.

The examinations which this book is planned to cover require the following knowledge as regards scales:

1. All major and all harmonic and melodic minor scales and their key signatures.
2. Simple and compound intervals within these scales.
3. Triads and their inversions on each note of the major and minor scales.
4. The harmonic chromatic scale.

MAJOR SCALES

These are formed of eight consecutive letter names, each letter name being used only once in any one scale, beginning on any note. The scale proceeds by an arrangement of tones and semitones, which must remain in the same order whatever note is used as the tonic or keynote. Thus in C major the pattern of two tetrachords each of two tones and one semitone, divided by one tone, is repeated in every other major scale, with sharps and flats added where necessary. The following diagram shows how these major scales are built. By discarding the first tetrachord of C major and adding a further one to the second tetrachord, all the sharp keys and then the flat keys follow in a logical sequence.

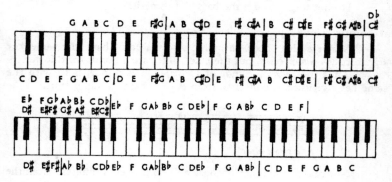

It will be noticed that C♯ major and D♭ major have exactly the same sound. This is called an enharmonic change, i.e. change of letter name, but not of note.

The *key signatures* are arranged for treble and bass clefs as follows:

C♯ major   G♭ major

(Although there could be a scale with seven flats beginning on C♭, it is rarely used, B major with five sharps on exactly the same notes being more convenient.)

If you wish to write the key signature of A major with three sharps, you will use the first three given in the previous example:

The key signature for A♭ with four flats would be the first four as taken from the example:

Practise writing all these scales with a row of widely spaced eight notes beginning on any tonic and then adding the proper sharps or flats:

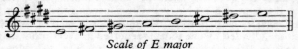

Scale of E major

Although it is not correct to have the key signature as well as the separate accidentals in front of the appropriate notes, it would be useful to add it for practice.

Do not forget to use the bass clef sometimes.

HARMONIC MINOR SCALES

Minor scales (both harmonic and melodic) have the same key signatures as major ones, but their key notes are a minor third lower.

Thus the *relative* minor of C major is A minor, both with the same key signature, the interval from A to C being a minor third:

A harmonic minor

Notice that the order of tones and semitones is different from the major scale.

In all harmonic minor scales the seventh note (the leading note) is raised one semitone. In the above example G must be changed to G♯. In the E♭ minor scale the seventh note, D♭, must become D♮. This alteration of the leading note does not affect the key signature, but only the note itself. Raising this seventh note by one semitone results in the distance between the sixth and seventh degrees becoming three semitones, or an augmented second, which we shall discuss later in relation to intervals.

This augmented second is also an important clue when assessing the key of a given melody or chord.

MELODIC MINOR SCALES

The use of the augmented second in harmonic minor scales was ungrateful for vocal melody, so the melodic minor is a variation to avoid this awkward leap.

The sixth and seventh degrees are raised one semitone ascending and lowered again one semitone when descending:

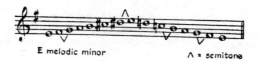

E melodic minor   ∧ = semitone

The key signature is unaffected by these accidentals.

Harmonic and melodic key signatures are as follows:

		Relative major
A minor has no sharps or flats	. . .	C
E minor has one sharp	. . .	G
B minor has two sharps	. . .	D
F♯ minor has three sharps	. . .	A
C♯ minor has four sharps	. . .	E
G♯ minor has five sharps	. . .	B
D♯ minor has six sharps	. . .	F♯
A♯ minor has seven sharps	. . .	C♯
D minor has one flat	. . .	F
G minor has two flats	. . .	B♭
C minor has three flats	. . .	E♭
F minor has four flats	. . .	A♭
B♭ minor has five flats	. . .	D♭
E♭ minor has six flats	. . .	G♭
A♭ minor has seven flats	. . .	C♭

The three minor scales of G♯, D♯ and A♯ are forced to have double sharps on their leading notes and are rarely used. The flat keys of A♭, E♭ and B♭ minor are more convenient, as they have the same sound, but do not need to employ such unusual accidentals. *See page 29*.

Practise writing these two minor scales with the *relative* major also, then with the *tonic* major, which begins on the same keynote, but which will have a different key signature (i.e. E minor has one sharp; E major has four sharps). Do not fail to notice that the main and invariable difference between the major and minor scales is the distance between the keynotes and their third and sixth degrees. The minor is always one semitone lower than the major.

The technical names for the degrees of all major and minor scales *must* be memorized, as many questions in examination papers are framed on this knowledge. They are as follows:

> 1st degree (keynote) is called the tonic
> 2nd degree is called the supertonic
> 3rd degree is called the mediant
> 4th degree is called the subdominant
> 5th degree is called the dominant
> 6th degree is called the submediant
> 7th degree is called the leading note
> 8th degree (again keynote) is called the tonic

Practise asking and answering yourself questions like these:

1. What is the submediant in the scales of C major, E minor, C♯ minor, etc.?
2. What is the supertonic of the same scales?

INTERVALS

An interval is the distance between two notes, always reckoning from the lower and counting it as number one.

Thus: is a 5th

They have five different names: major, minor, perfect, augmented and diminished.

You will notice in the list below that perfect intervals occur only from the tonic to the 4th and 5th degrees and to the octave. The major and minor intervals occur only from the tonic to the 2nd, 3rd, 6th and 7th degrees—the minor always being one semitone less than the major.

Augmented intervals are one semitone larger than the major or perfect and the diminished are one semitone less than minor or perfect.

The names of all the intervals which you will be required to recognize and write are as follows:

		Examples
Minor 2nd (1 semitone) .	. .	C to D♭
Major 2nd (2 semitones).	. .	C to D
Augmented 2nd (3 semitones).	. .	C to D♯
Minor 3rd (3 semitones).	. .	C to E♭
Major 3rd (4 semitones)	. .	C to E
Diminished 4th (4 semitones) .	. .	C to F♭
Perfect 4th (5 semitones)	. .	C to F
Augmented 4th (6 semitones) .	. .	C to F♯
Diminished 5th (6 semitones) .	. .	C to G♭
Perfect 5th (7 semitones)	. .	C to G
Augmented 5th (8 semitones) .	. .	C to G♯
Minor 6th (8 semitones).	. .	C to A♭

Major 6th (9 semitones) .   .   .   . C to A
Diminished 7th (9 semitones) .   .   .   . C to B♭♭
Minor 7th (10 semitones)   .   .   . C to B♭
Major 7th (11 semitones)   .   .   . C to B
Perfect 8th (octave) (12 semitones) .   .   . C to C

The frequent enharmonic changes (i.e. the same note called by another name) are necessary because of the variety of flat and sharp scales in which intervals occur.

Practise writing two plain notes on a stave and naming the interval; then add a sharp or a flat to either note and name it again. Also check in what scales it might occur. Example:

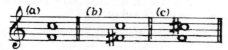

(*a*) is a perfect 5th occurring in F major, in C major (the lower note being the subdominant) in A minor (the lower note being the submediant) and in B♭ major (the lower note being the dominant).
(*b*) is a diminished 5th to be found in G minor, E minor and G major.
(*c*) is an augmented 5th to be found in D minor.

You may be asked to invert intervals. This is a mechanical and simple process. Examples:

F to A♭ is a minor 3rd
A♭ to F is a major 6th
G to D♯ is an augmented 5th
D♯ to G is a diminished 4th
F♯ to C♯ is a perfect 5th
C♯ to F♯ is a perfect 4th

When a minor interval is inverted it always becomes major
When a major interval is inverted it always becomes minor
When an augmented interval is inverted it always becomes diminished
When a diminished interval is inverted it always becomes augmented
When a perfect interval is inverted it always remains perfect

The value in numbers of degrees of the interval and its inversion always adds up to nine. These two kinds of results can be a valuable help in confirming the correctness of your judgment about the original intervals.

The accidental before the leading note in harmonic minor scales is included in the assessment of intervals. Thus F♯ to C♯ is a perfect 5th occurring in the scale of D major. F♮ to C♯ is an augmented 5th occurring in the scale of D minor.

In judging the key of a melody, chord or modulation, the apparent discrepancy of the use of C♯, with no F♯, should point to a strong possibility that the example may be in the key of D minor.

Intervals within one octave are called simple. Intervals beyond an octave are called compound, but they are merely an extension of simple intervals.

Example of compound interval:

Major 10th.

TRIADS AND THEIR INVERSIONS

Triads are composed of three notes, and when inverted the original lowest note remains the root. Example:

Root position — 1st Inversion — 2nd Inversion

G remains the root of this major triad in both inversions.

A triad can be built on each degree of any major scale, adding the 3rd and 5th degrees above, and will be found to vary between major, minor and diminished.

Thus, on the scale of D major:

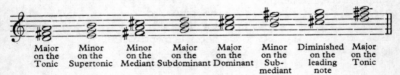

Major on the Tonic — Minor on the Supertonic — Minor on the Mediant — Major on the Subdominant — Major on the Dominant — Minor on the Sub-mediant — Diminished on the leading note — Major on the Tonic

It will be noted that the 3rd governs the choice between major and minor, except for the triad on the leading note, in which the 3rd is minor and the 5th, C♯ to G, is a diminished interval. In all the others the 5th is perfect.

The triads found upon the degrees of the harmonic minor scale (the melodic is not used for this purpose) are as follows:
On the scale of D minor:

Minor — Diminished — Augmented — Minor — Major — Major — Diminished — Minor

Notice that again the 3rd governs the choice between major and minor where the 5th is perfect. But if the 5th changes to diminished or augmented then the triad will receive those names.

Practise writing triads on selected degrees of major and minor scales in root position only, such as:

(a) on the dominant in A major
(b) on the leading note in G major
(c) on the supertonic in C minor
(d) on the medient in F minor

and state whether major, minor, diminished or augmented.

You will see that triads often occur in more than one scale, as intervals did. For instance:

(a) can be found also in E major on the tonic and in B major on the subdominant.
(b) can be found in E minor on the supertonic.
(c) can be found in E♭ major and in E♭ minor on the leading note.
(d) can be found only in F minor.

The inversion of triads is a simple procedure.

(a) Triad on the tonic of C minor:

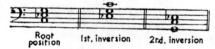

(b) Triad on the mediant of C minor:

Practise writing inversions in the following way:

Write the first inversion of the subdominant triad in E♭ major (C, E♭, A♭).

Write the second inversion of the supertonic triad in D minor (B♭, E, G).

Write the root position of the mediant triad in F♯ major (A♯, C♯ and E♯).

Do not confuse 'tonic' with 'root'.

The tonic is the keynote of a scale, while root is the lowest note of a triad in root position. In example (b) above the root of these three triads is E♭ in each case, but they do not include the tonic at all, which, of course, is C.

THE HARMONIC CHROMATIC SCALE

  This includes all notes used on Western instruments going up or down by semitone all the way. To write these scales in an orderly way, start on any chosen note or tonic, leave a space of about one and a half inches, then write a perfect 5th from your tonic. Leave another slightly shorter space and then write the tonic again an octave higher.

  Now fill in *two* of every other note by spaces and lines in between these three notes. Then add sharps or flats to complete every semitone without missing a single one.

  Thus the harmonic chromatic scale of D:

Practise starting on *any* note, using this method. Always check carefully that you have made no small mistake.

TRANSPOSING FROM ONE KEY TO ANOTHER

  This process has three stages:
1. To determine the key of the given piece.
2. To determine the new key and the exact interval dividing it from the old one.
3. To write your music as neatly as possible and to check very carefully for small mistakes.

  1. The key signature at the beginning of the given piece will allow two alternatives, major or minor. Perhaps you cannot decide definitely if the final note is the tonic. (It *could* be the 3rd or even the 5th —although most probably it *will* be the tonic.) Then look for an accidental, which might be the 7th note of a minor key. For instance, if a key signature of two flats is given, look for an F♯, which might show you that it was in G minor.

  2. Perhaps you will be asked to transpose the given piece an augmented 4th higher. (Remember, if the first piece is major it will remain major and minor will remain minor.) If it is in F major, that would take you up to B major, F to B♮ being an augmented 4th. This will give you your new key signature of five sharps.

  Now take the first note of the given piece and transpose it up an augmented 4th. If it was C it will now be F♯, but the sharp will be indicated by the new key signature, so, of course, you will not add it to the note itself.

  Proceed by copying exactly the same pattern of notes four letter names apart.

It is a firm rule that you will need an accidental only where it occurs in the original piece, and each one must be considered separately and carefully, as a sharp in the first piece need not necessarily be a sharp in the transposition. If a note is raised or lowered a semitone it might have to be a natural when transposed. For example:

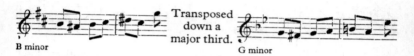

B minor   Transposed down a major third.   G minor

3. In the empty stave provided for your transposition, first write the clef required, then the new key signature and the old time signature, which, of course, remains the same.

Then draw the bar lines exactly where they occur in the first piece and that will guide you to tidy spacing of your new version, with the notes well apart and not crowded up together like a drawing of some rather muddled knitting! It is a good idea to write just the note heads first and to add the tails later. Otherwise you may find yourself mechanically copying a group of quavers with turned-up tails far too high on the stave. Don't forget to copy all phrase and expression marks and take a pride in drawing your manuscript music as beautifully as you can.

TRANSPOSING INTO ANOTHER CLEF

The most used clefs are the treble and bass, with the alto clef always in use for the viola, and, with the tenor clef, occasionally in use for some orchestral instruments. (See Chapter on The Orchestra.) Here are the Cs on each clef:

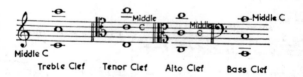

Treble Clef   Tenor Clef   Alto Clef   Bass Clef

Take note of the position of middle C in each example, and when transposing from one to another be careful to remain at the same level of pitch, unless asked to do otherwise.

Treble   into   Tenor

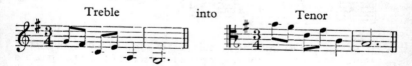

Accidentals do not alter in transposing from one clef to another. They always remain exactly the same.

REDUCTION OF AN EXCERPT FROM A STRING QUARTET SCORE TO PIANO SCORE
AND THE REVERSE

Reduction cannot, of course, reproduce the sustained quality of strings or wind instruments or of voices, but it can be a most useful exercise for studying the harmonic and melodic structure of a composer's work, and in more difficult modern music can clarify some sounds which the not-very-experienced eye would be unable to translate from score to ear.

To make the reduction is a mechanical process, except for attention to the transposing of the viola part, which should be taken from the alto clef and carefully re-written at the same pitch in the bass clef.

Retain each separate part intact by turning the tails up for violin I part and down for violin II on the treble stave, up for the viola part and down for the 'cello on the bass stave. Even if the parts cross, the tails should keep this pattern.

Here is a short example from the String Quartet No. 2 in F sharp by Michael Tippett:

Should you be studying the solo part of a piano quintet, quartet or trio, to be able to reduce the string parts for a second pianist to practise with you on another piano is a useful accomplishment. Or perhaps your solo instrument is the clarinet? If so, find a miniature score of Brahms quintet for clarinet in A and strings, op. 115, and try reducing a couple of pages of the adagio movement for solo clarinet and piano. Here is how it begins and how it should be arranged:

The clarinet sounds a minor third lower than written, so its first actual note here would sound as F♯. (See Chapter on The Orchestra.)

In the reverse process of arranging a four-part piano piece in open score for string quartet, the only special requirement is for the upper part in the left hand to be transposed into the alto clef for the viola, and for care to be taken that the notes of each part are neatly perpendicular as when printed. (See example of Tippett quartet in open score.)

MODES

The names of the six Greek modes referred to on page 18 and using the white notes only of the keyboard are:

Ionian C–C	Lydian F–F
Dorian D–D	Mixolydian G–G
Phrygian E–E	Aeolian A–A

It will be noted that the order of tones and semitones differ in each scale.

DOUBLE SHARPS, DOUBLE FLATS AND THEIR CONTRADICTIONS

A double sharp, written X, raises the note two semitones.

A double flat, written ♭♭, lowers the note two semitones.

To restore a note to one sharp substitute a single sharp, and the same for one flat.

To discard the X or ♭♭ altogether substitute a single natural.

CHAPTER FOUR

Rhythmic and Melodic Aural Tests

The recognition of intervals, cadences and chords

RHYTHMIC DICTATION

THE RECOGNITION OF ONLY relatively simple rhythms is expected. Try to establish, the very first time the examiner plays the example you have to write down by ear, whether it is *simple* or *compound* in pattern. It is possible to confuse $\frac{3}{4}$ and $\frac{6}{8}$ if no quavers are used in the $\frac{3}{4}$ example, but that would be very unlikely.

Notice how the groupings of two quavers to a beat establishes $\frac{3}{4}$ in the first of the following examples:

Practise tapping these two examples with the accents marked. The examiner may play the rhythm example as a *melody*, but this should help you to remember, and repeat it to yourself silently after he has finished playing. He will probably give a *slightly* heavier accent on the first beat of each bar, and that you must carefully note—filling in the weaker pulses in between. You will be able to start writing rough notes as soon as he has begun to play.

MELODIC AURAL TESTS

Most students, if given a key note in the lower part of their vocal range, can hum a major scale correctly because most of the music we hear is built on this or the minor scale and our ears have become completely indoctrinated. But if we think for a moment about the construction of tones and semitones which form the major scale we realize that this ability is based only on habit and not on a conscious adjustment of two tones, one semitone, three tones and one semitone which actually form the major scale.

We must *know* what is being heard and be able to write it down on a stave. Begin by getting into a quiet corner and humming or singing the following chromatic scale:

that is, using every semitone twice except the tonic. This can help to establish a safer feeling for semitones. Then attempt to pitch each note in turn from the tonic.

Now try humming the following scale, which is composed of six whole tones:

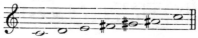

To pitch the 5th and 6th of this scale from the tonic will need much practice. Follow this by humming a major scale and noting where the semitones occur. Then try the melodic minor scale, and after that the harmonic minor, which introduces a new interval, the augmented 2nd, one semitone larger than a whole tone. Also pitch all these notes from the tonic. Now practise singing the intervals listed on p. 22, noting the various technical names of each one. It is most important to be able to create your own intervals vocally and not merely to recognize them when played on the piano.

For examination purposes you will be required to listen to a short major or minor melody played four or five times, of which the key and time signature will probably be stated in advance, on these lines:

Then you must write it. The first bar would be easy, but the minor 7th (G♯ to F♯) in the second bar is more difficult until you realize that it slips up to the tonic. In fact, tracing the course of a melody is a mixture of quick appreciation of intervals and a strong feeling for the tonic. For instance, in bars 3 and 4 in the above example, the perfect 5th (F♯ to C♯) will be confirmed by the last three notes proceeding to the tonic.

Begin practising for this question by asking a second person to

play some very easy phrases for you like these, telling you the key and
time signatures first:

You may also be given dictation of a *two-part phrase* comprising, perhaps,
about four or five intervals played harmonically, not melodically.

The examiner will play the passages at least four times each, having
already given you the key and time signatures. He will also precede each
play-through with the tonic chord, which should greatly help towards
finding your first note in both parts, that being the immediate concern.
On the second hearing, try to confirm the top part. Then concentrate on
the lower part. It is possible that the phrase will not end on the tonic chord
(in this case on the dominant), so do not be deceived. Also it commences
in the upper part on the 3rd, and in the lower part on the 5th, neither
being the key note, as you might expect.

CADENCES

You will be asked to recognize the four cadences, perfect, plagal,
imperfect and interrupted, as played at the end of four short, separate

phrases of four or five four-part chords *or* one continuous musical sentence containing two or more selected cadences.

You will not have to write the actual notes; only the names of the cadences. Your attention should be on the tonic chord which will precede each example, and then firmly directed to the bass part which will technically determine the cadences. From listening to them many times during your studies you will appreciate the special sound or colour of each cadence and that will help a great deal.

Here are a few examples:

Study these yourself first and then ask a second person to play them while you listen. After that, the more frequently you can persuade a fellow student to play other examples for you, the better! They will be in major or minor keys.

RECOGNITION OF CHORDS

This series of four or five four-part chords will be root positions and their inversions in any major or minor key.

The chords to be named will probably be tonic, supertonic, sub-dominant, dominant and submediant, and possibly in their first or second inversions. In addition, the dominant 7th may be played, which you will have practised writing during your study of the chapter on harmony.

This is a typical example:

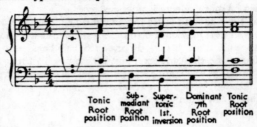

Tonic   Sub-mediant   Super-tonic   Dominant   Tonic
Root position   Root position   1st. inversion   7th Root position   Root position

Again, after specially noting the tonic chord, the bass part should be sketched down on your rough paper. Then you must decide if any of the chords are inversions. During your study of the four-part harmony you will be learning to write and to *hear* (we *insist*!) the simple progressions which are contained in these aural tests.

There is really no short cut to familiarity with the sound and recognition of these chords. They must be listened to many times, always in relation to the tonic chord, which does reduce the number of tone colours to be remembered.

SIMPLE MODULATION

You will be required to recognize and name modulations in a harmonic passage. The key and the tonic chord will be named and played first.

There will be only one modulation in any one passage, and these will be limited to modulations to the dominant, subdominant and relative major or minor keys. Here are some examples:

Tonic to subdominant   Tonic to dominant

Major to relative minor   Minor to relative major

You will notice that a note foreign to the original key will be introduced to herald the modulation, and it will be the dominant 7th of the new key. This will be preceded by a pivot chord which is one common to both old and new keys. Try to note down the bass part of the few chords involved, especially noticing the interval between the bass note of the final chord and the tonic: that should confirm your decision as to the new key.

COMPOSING A MELODY TO GIVEN WORDS

In setting words to a melody the rhythm of the verse must first be established. It may fit to various time patterns—but one of the simple or compound time signatures must be selected to which the heavy and light accents of the words appear to be best suited. First underline the heavy accents.

> The JABberwock with EYES of flame
>
> Came WHIFfling through the TULgey wood
>
> And BURbled as it CAME.

Then put bar lines before the accents and add simple note values:

The | JABberwock with | EYES of flame

Came | WHIFfling through the | TUL-gey wood

And | | BURbled as it | CAME

The choice of $\frac{4}{4}$ time is stolid, but it is not incorrect. If you prefer the lilt of $\frac{6}{8}$, then that is equally possible. Having established the time signature and the gist of the words, consider the sense in relation to the sound you want to produce for the melody.

This poem, of course, is a kind of nonsense verse and the sounds could therefore be a little comic, but do not write anything—not one single note—that you cannot actually hear inside your head.

If you first decide what voice you wish to use, that will tell you the range you can attempt and might possibly help in choosing your key.

The average compass of human voices for practical purposes is as follows:

(*a*) Use the extreme notes sparingly. The vocal lines for tenor and baritone voices are usually written in the treble clef—one octave higher. Songs for a bass voice are often written in the bass clef, and it would be correct to do that. Now count the number of bars and plan where you could modulate if you wish to do so. It would most likely occur somewhere in the second line, to (*a*) establish the chosen key, (*b*) pass through a pivot chord common to both past and future key, (*c*) introduce the dominant 7th chord of a new key, (*d*) establish a new key (which in this case is the dominant of the old key), and (*e*) return to the old original key by adding the minor 7th.

(*b*) Here is an example in D major for a baritone voice, worked in stages. There are six bars and I prefer the 6 rhythm. It is intended to modulate to the dominant key and back again.

Rhythmic framework

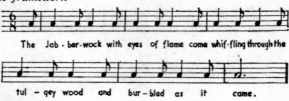

Implied harmonies

Tune based on implied harmonies

As there are no chords to confirm the harmonies, the tune should use the notes of each implied chord to give clarity. But this is a very plain melody, so with some passing notes and slight alteration of layout, without disturbing the implied harmonies, it could be made a little more suitable to the verse. When setting words, it is a good idea to remember that singers must breathe and to arrange to have rests at intervals! You will also make use of the expression and speed marks you have learnt. Phrase the passage and indicate an overall direction of style and speed.

Notice the conventions of writing for voices. When a syllable has more than one note attached to it the notes should be joined with a slur and the syllable itself followed by a - (as in 'whiffling' above). A word which is broken and spaced on to separate notes, (as 'tulgey' above) should also have a hyphen. Voices can crescendo and decrescendo very well, and most especially on held notes, so make use of such possibilities.

TO COMPLETE A MELODY

First decide *how much* of the piece you have been given ready made—that is, in rhythmic terms. Tap the note values out and add the number of bars necessary to complete the framework.

If you were given this:

and then tapped the rhythm you might find yourself continuing something like this:

That falls naturally into eight bars.

Perhaps you will be asked to modulate into the relative minor and then finish in the tonic again. Decide what key you are in, and then work out a plan of chord changes to cover your modulation instructions.

Now your tune can spring out of these necessary harmonies. Be sure that you hear the given fragment correctly. Take great care that all intervals are exact and, if it is a minor key, be positive that your 3rd is a minor one.

You will be expected to be conventional in the shaping of your phrases: *i.e.* they should have similar patterns and not shoot off into some completely fresh idea which has no possibility of proper development.

Here is a simple modulation on the chord plan given above:

The changes are negotiated with a pivot chord, followed by new leading note (D♯) to relative minor key of E. C major then acts as pivot chord back to G major with leading note (F♯) to confirm it immediately preceding the tonic.

♩=60 means a crotchet beat matched to the 60-mark tick of a metronome, which is similar to the tick of a grandfather clock.

CHAPTER FIVE

Two-part Harmony or the Dual Melodic Line

(*This should be taken in conjunction with four-part harmony*)

1. EACH PART SHOULD MAKE a good contrapuntal line. Look at the following excerpt from Handel's *Messiah*.

2. Intervals to be used are major and minor 3rds and 6ths, unison, octave and the perfect 5th.

3. Both parts should end with the tonic chord.

4. Parts should move in contrary motion whenever possible.

5. Consecutive 5ths and octaves are forbidden.

6. The octave or unison may be used as follows:

   (*a*) At the beginning or end or both.

   (*b*) On the dominant or at the final cadence.

   (*c*) On a weak beat:

      1. Between two positions of the same chord, both parts moving by step and in contrary motion.

2. When the notes forming the octave belong to the same chord as that used on the previous strong beat.

9. The perfect 5th may be used as follows:
   (*a*) At the beginning, over the tonic or dominant.

(*b*) On a weak beat when the upper part moves by step between the tonic and mediant or *vice versa* or between the subdominant and submediant.

(*c*) On the dominant of the final cadence.

10. Parts may be written on separate staves or together on a single stave; in the latter case the notes of the upper parts will have their stems upwards, those of the lower parts downwards.

11. When writing in two parts, learn to think in keys. See, for instance, the Minuet in G major in the book by Bach for his wife, Anna Magdalena. The middle section, after the double bar, is in D major. The piece then modulates back to G major. Also note that it is easier for the beginner to use the harmonic minor scale, but avoid augmented intervals.

12. AUXILIARY NOTES

(a) *Upper auxiliary note** or upper mordent. This may be a note next above a chord note and formed from any note of the scale commencing with the root of the chord.

(b) *Lower auxiliary note** or lower mordent. Usually one semitone below the chord note.

13. Use a good bass and independent motion of the parts. See the following Romance in G for violin by Beethoven.

(a) Contrary motion.
(b) Similar motion.
(c) Oblique motion.

14. Parts need not be written note for note with each other. See also the examples by Bach and Mendelssohn on page 60. These examples are in florid two-part writing, which is not actually required for G.C.E. 'O' Level.

N.B.—Do not continue unessential notes beyond a cadence point.

15. As a general rule, notes which are the same may be tied (a) to give a feeling of suspense, but the use of (b) suspensions themselves

should be restricted to those resolving on the intervals of the 3rd and the 6th. Both these create SYNCOPATION.

Note: The suspension need not be tied, but can be struck with a harmony note to form a dissonance, thereby creating interest. See the Two-part Inventions by J. S. Bach for two-part writing. See also string writing in Chapter on The Orchestra.

CHAPTER SIX

Elementary Four-part Harmony

HISTORICALLY, the first phase of harmony seems to have been traditional plainsong sung in octaves. Later, probably in the ninth and tenth centuries, it became the practice to double the plainsong at intervals of the 4th and 5th. This was called ORGANUM.

Next developed an early type of counterpoint, which probably began with an improvised descant over the original melody, or CANTO FERMO. This opened up a great expansion of available resources and gradually led to the modern key system and abandonment of the modes.

Text-book harmony, as required for examinations, is based on the rules of a fairly limited period in harmonic writing—that is, the seventeenth and eighteenth centuries. The following is an attempt to put these rules simply and clearly. However, in order to unite practice with theory, some examples are included to show where to find these harmonic rules in the compositions of great composers, as well as carols and ordinary folk-music. The student is urged to find many more for himself. Compositions in which composers break rules are also referred to.

The student is also urged to play and listen to all the chords and progressions in the harmony examples as well as to write them down from dictation.

The teacher will be able to supply many more examples and set exercises for the student at every stage. (*108 Exercises in Harmonization*, by W. Lovelock, published by Hammond & Co., is a useful book.)

TRIADS

We have seen in a previous chapter on scales the method of building up triads on the major and minor diatonic scale. The table below should be learnt by the student so that he can distinguish any chord when it is played after the sounding of the tonic chord.

The *primary* triads, I, IV and V, are the most simple to use, *and should be learnt first*.

The *secondary* triads, II and VI in major and VI in minor can be used for elementary harmony.

Another secondary triad, III, in the major key should not be used at present.

VII in major and II, III and VII in minor are discords, and should not be used at the moment.

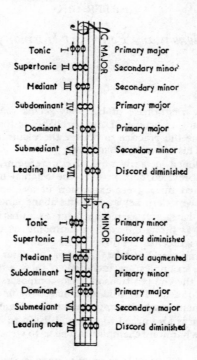

Tonic	I	Primary major
Supertonic	II	Secondary minor
Mediant	III	Secondary minor
Subdominant	IV	Primary major
Dominant	V	Primary major
Submediant	VI	Secondary minor
Leading note	VII	Discord diminished

C MAJOR

Tonic	I	Primary minor
Supertonic	II	Discord diminished
Mediant	III	Discord augmented
Subdominant	IV	Primary minor
Dominant	V	Primary major
Submediant	VI	Secondary major
Leading note	VII	Discord diminished

C MINOR

The following harmony arrangement is for four voices, two in the treble and two in the bass.

The $\frac{5}{3}$ chord has its two upper notes a 5th and a 3rd from the bass and is called a 'root chord'.

The $\frac{6}{3}$ chord has its two upper notes a 6th and a 3rd from the bass and is called a 'first inversion'.

The $\frac{6}{4}$ chord has its two upper notes a 6th and a 4th from the bass and is called a 'second inversion'.

Note: The major 3rd should not be doubled, although the bass and 5th may be. The minor 3rd may be doubled. The leading note **should never be doubled**.

Omission of the 3rd. The 5th may be omitted, but never the 3rd. Beethoven disregarded this rule in the opening of the Ninth Symphony, however, thereby creating an atmosphere of dim vastness.

RULES FOR CHORD PROGRESSIONS

The $\frac{5}{3}$ chord or chord in root position.

1. Note the direction of the tails in all parts. These directions must be strictly adhered to in order to avoid confusion between the parts.

2. The compass of the parts is as follows:

3. Parts should not cross, i.e. S (soprano) is highest, A (alto) next highest, T (tenor) next, and B (bass) is lowest.

4. In order to make the melody interesting, it is a good plan to write the S first, then B, and then add A and T. If the bass only is given, add first the soprano, choosing any note of the chord, and then the middle parts.

5. If a soprano note is given with A, T, B, to be added below, it may belong to more than one chord, so that more than one harmonization may be possible. For instance, in C major a soprano C can be the root of I, the 5th of IV or the 3rd of VI, thus:

6. (*a*) No part may leap any augmented interval, i.e. augmented 2nd, 4th, the tritone or 5th:

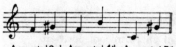

Augmented 2nd. Augmented 4th. Augmented 5th.

(*b*) No part may leap a 7th or 9th, nor any larger interval nor with one note between.

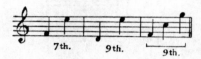

7th. 9th. 9th.

7. (*a*) A part may leap a diminished 5th, provided it is followed by a leap *within* the interval.

Good Bad

(*b*) The same applies to the 6th and the octave.

6th. Octave

8. Leaps of a 4th and 7th should be avoided at present.

9. The leading note should rise to the tonic in progressions V-I and V-VI.

V   I   V   VI

10. No two parts may move in parallel or contrary perfect 5ths or octaves.

Puccini breaks this rule in *Tosca*, Act I, andante lento in F major bars 3, 4 and 5, etc.

11. (*a*) S and B may not approach an octave or 5th in similar motion with a leap in the S. This is called an 'exposed octave'. The S must approach by step.

(*b*) When the 3rd of II falls to the 5th of V the exposed 5th between II and V is allowable.

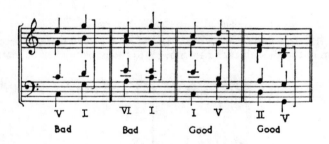

12. Keep identical notes occurring in two consecutive chords in the same part if possible.

13. In passing from one chord to another each chord should normally move to the nearest available part, although not always when

taking the leading note to the tonic. The 5th may be omitted, but the 3rd not.

14. Do not overlap parts except between two positions of the same chord.

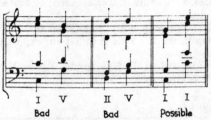

15. In using IV-V or V-IV, the S, A, T should move in contrary motion to the B, with each part moving to the nearest available note.

16. In using V-VI, the 3rd of VI should be doubled as it is approached by steps in contrary motion. In VI-V the 3rd of VI is also doubled as it is being quitted by steps in contrary motion.

This rule may be disregarded in the major key, except where V-VI is used as a cadence.

17. *The perfect cadence or full close, V-I.* This is the final resting point in music and should only be written at the beginning or end of a set of harmonic progressions. In every case the leading note rises to the tonic. (Bach and other writers sometimes allow the leading note to fall.)

See Mozart's Sonata for piano in G major (K.283). Presto, end of first section, bars 101 and 102. Note the music has modulated to the dominant—a perfect cadence in D major.

See Beethoven's Sonata, op. 10, no. 1, last three bars of the first movement, ending in a perfect cadence in the tonic key of C major.

Note: This is piano music and therefore four-part vocal writing rules do not apply.

This cadence is in a minor key, ending with a major chord. It is called *Tierce de Picardie*. Up to Bach's time all pieces in minor were automatically finished in major in this way.

Note the major end to this fugue by Bach, no. 2 in C minor, Book I, *Forty-eight Preludes and Fugues*.

Note the magnificent way Bach repeats the subject once more over the tonic pedal note of C before the major ending. (A pedal note is usually in the bass and sustained through a succession of harmonies.)

PLAGAL CADENCE

18. Another final resting-point, this is more to be found amongst

hymn tunes and carols than in the works of nineteenth-century composers.

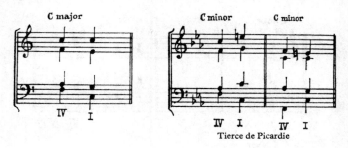

See 'The First Noel', bars 3 and 4, but even here note its position at the end of the first phrase, with the tonic chord in its first inversion.

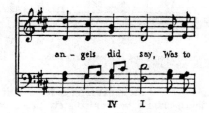

INTERRUPTED CADENCE

19. V-VI non-final. Instances may be found in Bach's Ab major fugue, Book II, *Forty-eight Preludes and Fugues*, bar 43; Mozart's Violin Sonata (K.454), second movement at bars 14 and 18; Mozart's Symphony in Eb, fourth movement, bar 52; Beethoven's Piano Sonata, op. 10, no. 3, fourth movement, bars 6 and 7.

IMPERFECT CADENCE OR HALF CLOSE, NON-FINAL

    20. *Note:* II–V is not available in the minor keys.

(*a*) See 'O Come all ye faithful', bars 1 and 2; (*b*) Mozart's Rondo from Piano Sonata in C, bars 3–4; (*c*) See hymn tune 'Rockingham'.

The student is urged to find the remaining cadence points for himself.

    21. No cadence should be immediately preceded by its second chord, nor should the first chord be repeated twice even if differently arranged.

ROOTS

    22. Roots of chords a 4th or 5th apart are a strong progression. Roots falling a 3rd are good. Roots rising a 3rd are only good from a strong to a weak accent.

    23. IV–V–I is a good and usual progression.

    24. No chord may be repeated weak to strong except at the beginning of a sentence, and if a melody note is repeated or tied the chord should be changed on the repetition. Also avoid repetition with one chord in between.

FIRST INVERSION OF TRIADS

    This is called the $\frac{6}{3}$ chord.

    1. When the chord has the 3rd in the bass it is in its first inversion and the letter 'b' is added after its number, e.g. Ib. Note the addition of

VIIb to the chords now available in major and IIb and VIIb in minor.
This is in addition to those in root position.

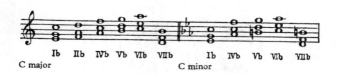

2. DOUBLING

Major keys. Double the 3rd and 6th above the bass, but not the
bass itself.

Minor keys. Any of the notes may be doubled.

Do not double the leading note.

3. Do not omit any note of the chord.

4. FIRST INVERSIONS MOVING BY STEP

The soprano and alto move in parallel 3rds and 6ths with the bass.
The tenor alternately doubles the 6th and the 3rd.

5. A perfect 5th followed by a diminished 5th or *vice versa* may
be used between *upper* parts, but not in the bass.

6. The following points should be carefully memorized:

(*a*) Avoid VIIb-V, VIIb-IVa and VIIb-IVb if possible. VIIb-I or Ib
is the best.

(*b*) Vb sounds best if followed by Ia or VIb with leading note to tonic
in the bass.

(*c*) Double the bass of IIb on IIb-Va if possible.

(*d*) VIIb-I or Ib. Let parts move by step if possible.

7. CADENCES

New forms available are:

Perfect Cadences

Imperfect Cadences

Ib V   IIb V   VIb V   IVb V

Written here in a major key, but also available in minor.

8. If the bass has the first three notes of the scale descending, use Ib-VIIb-I or *vice versa*.

Ib VIIb I   I   VIIb Ib

Note the alternative arrangements of S, A, T.

9. Note the following points for harmonization:

(*a*) Avoid ungainly leaps, too many consecutive leaps and remaining round one pitch for too long. It is no longer necessary to adhere strictly to the principle of moving to the nearest note, but the writing should be kept within bounds and the melody have a good curve.

(*b*) Use a good, melodious bass.

(*c*) V-Ib or Vb-I makes for greater fluency than Va-Ia if a dominant to tonic harmony is required in the opening.

(*d*) Changing from root position to first inversion of the same chord is only good from a strong to weak accent.

For passages in inversions by a great composer see Beethoven's Sonatas for Pianoforte, op. 2, no. 3, fourth movement.

Now look at bars 23 to 28 of the same movement.

Also see Sonata, op. 7, first movement, bars 59-65, in the first section, and in the same movement, second section, bars 187-191 from the double bar.

SECOND INVERSIONS OF TRIADS: THE $\frac{6}{4}$ CHORD

1. The 5th of the root is in the bass, and the letter 'c' is added after its number.

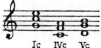

2. THE CADENTIAL $\frac{6}{4}$

(a) Only Ic and IVc are possible, and the first one is most used.

(b) They proceed to the $\frac{5}{3}$ from the same bass, the 6th falls to the 5th and the 4th to the 3rd. The remaining part doubles the bass.

(c) Do not accent the $\frac{5}{3}$ more strongly than the $\frac{6}{4}$.

(d) The bass of the $\frac{6}{4}$ must not be approached by a leap from the *inversion* of another chord.

3. If the final bass note lasts three beats, the IVc Cadential can be used to decorate a Plagal Cadence.

Here are some examples from compositions of great composers. Beethoven, op. 2, no. 1, second movement, Adagio:

Mozart, Sonata in A (K.331)

IIb Ic V7 I

4. THE PASSING $\frac{6}{4}$

Only Ic and Vc are possible.

IVb Ic IV   IV Ic IVb   Ib Vc I   I Vc Ib

(*a*) The $\frac{6}{4}$ is always on a weak beat and the bass moves by step.

(*b*) The 5th note of the scale in the soprano should be unaccented.

5. The last two examples should preferably replace the progressions on page 54 (last examples) provided that the middle chord is unaccented. If it *is* accented, use VIIb.

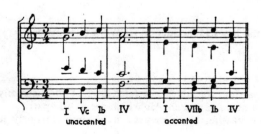

I Vc Ib IV   I VIIb Ib IV
unaccented   accented

Here is the passing $\frac{6}{4}$ chord in actual music:

Note the key has modulated from B♭ to F major.

UNACCENTED PASSING NOTES

1. A passing note does not form part of the harmony and may come between notes of any chords which are a 3rd apart.

2. Two passing notes may be used simultaneously in different

parts, provided they move in *parallel* 3rds and 6ths. (Do not use more than two passing notes at a time.)

3. Provided they are an octave apart, two parts may take the same passing note simultaneously.

4. Passing notes and harmony may only be struck together when they form a concord:

5. Avoid minor 9ths and 5ths.

In minor keys the 4th, as an unessential note, may be sounded against the 3rd as a harmony note.

6. Avoid running one part into another or having parts running too close together.

7. The 6th of the scale as a passing note is sharpened, but the 7th is not. This avoids the augmented 2nd.

8. When using passing notes, do not harmonize quavers with

crotchet beats, crotchets with minim beats or semiquavers with quaver beats. This makes for congestion.

9. In triple time, do not harmonize only the first and second beats of the bar. This principle also applies to compound time.

Examples from the great masters:

See also chapter on two-part writing, point 14.

THE DOMINANT 7TH

1. This is the dominant triad with the minor 7th above the root added. It is called V7 and the figuring is $\frac{7}{5}$.
$\frac{}{3}$

V7

2. As this is a discord, it needs resolution.

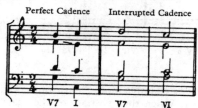

(a) The 7th above the root should fall a step to chords I or VI.
(b) The 5th from the root may be omitted.
(c) The 3rd is doubled in VI as usual.
(d) In harmonizing a cadence, introduce the 7th as late as possible.

This is a perfect cadence.

3. In root position the dominant 7th can resolve to IVb or IVc, the 7th being kept in the same part.

4. The three inversions all resolve to the tonic chord.

(a) Inversions must be complete.

(b) If the bass to Ib rises a step the 7th also rises a step (examples below).

These are all perfect cadences:

In the following example, note the use of the 7th kept as the same note weak to strong. When the 4th note of the scale is tied and falls a step it *must* be harmonized as V7d.

5. The cadential $\frac{6}{4}$ (Ic) may be followed by V7d provided the 4th is not stronger than the 5th.

6. Ornamental resolution of perfect cadences. The 7th moves to the 5th of the chord before resolving.

V7b   I   V7c   I

So many instances of the use of the dominant 7th, both in passing and cadentially, appear in the works of great composers that the student is urged to make investigations for himself. See especially Beethoven's Sonatas for Pianoforte.

ACCENTED PASSING NOTES (THE APPOGGIATURA)

1. These are on the strong or accented part of the beat and proceed to the harmony note of the beat afterwards.

2. An accented passing note and its note of resolution may not be struck together unless the latter is in the bass, but the following are also correct.

VI   VIb   VIIb   I   Ib   V

3. (*a*) Accented passing notes ascending should move in parallel 3rds and 6ths between the root and 3rd and 3rd and 5th of the same chord.

(*b*) This also applies when descending.

I   IVb   I   Ib   IV

4. Two parts may take the same accented note in contrary motion at least an octave apart.

ACCENTED PASSING NOTES IN THE BASS

5. Do not move from the bass of the second inversion.

6. If there is a leap to another chord the note before the leap must be a harmony note.

This applies to any part.

7. In a descending scalic passage, use accented passing notes instead of unaccented ones. The accented discord always gives an impression of movement forwards.

The accented passing note was found very useful by composers to express passion and drama with great intensity.

Beethoven: Sonata, op. 81a
Andante espressivo

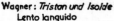

Wagner: *Tristan und Isolde*
Lento languido

Accented passing notes

SUSPENSIONS

1. A suspension, much less dramatic than the accented passing note, occurs when the note is held back from its resolution, e.g.

(*a*) Note that the second crotchet C in the second bar should have occurred on the first beat.

(*b*) The second of the two tied (or played) notes should not last longer than the first.

2. A suspension may occur in any part and any note of a triad may be suspended.

3. The notes of the resolution may not be sounded unless the former be in the bass (as in accented passing notes).

4. The suspension of the 5th of the chord is only effective when used with the second inversion, as only thus is the necessary discord created and the interest maintained.

5. Suspensions in the bass. At this stage it is safest to suspend

only the 3rd. The note of resolution may *not* be sounded above the suspension.

6. A suspension may resolve into another position of the same chord (*a*) or into another chord (*b*) provided that the chord contains the note of resolution. The suspended note should fall a step. Avoid consecutives.

7. Avoid this: Drop the E to C

8. A double suspension is possible if two notes fall together into a chord in parallel 3rds and 6ths.

9. An upward resolving suspension is called a retardation. This is best used together with a downward falling suspension, usually a 4th falling to a 3rd. The retardation is usually the leading note to the tonic.

10. Suspensions can be used with the root, 3rd and 5th of the dominant 7th.

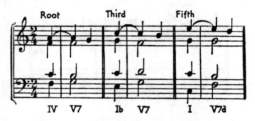

11. The following are possible ornamental resolutions:

Examples from great composers:

Retardations or upward resolving suspensions.

Note modulation to C major at X and suspended leading note.

ELEMENTARY MODULATION

The idea of using various keys in one composition was a fairly late development in Western music and only came into practice after the old modal way of writing had been finally dropped. However, from the seventeenth century onwards this practice was more and more developed until composers felt they could modulate, i.e. change gradually and easily, into *any* key they chose.

However, the earliest modulations were from tonic to dominant, and the student should first attempt to grasp the feeling of this both theoretically and aurally, e.g.

1. *Pivot modulation* (gradual).

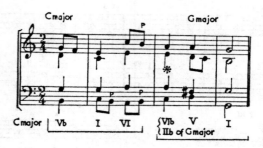

* *Pivot chord.* This is the 6th chord of the scale of C major and the 2nd chord of the scale of G major, e.g. chord of A minor. (*Note:* When a note of the old key is chromatically altered into the new it should not appear in the same part.)

2. The appearance of a new note belonging to the new key but not the old and a cadence in a new key mark a modulation.

3. A sharpened note is generally the leading note of a new key. It may also be the supertonic of a new key.

4. A flattened note is usually the subdominant of a new key (harmonized as the 7th of V7). Note the following from actual compositions:

Handel : *Messiah*

* Pivot chord between keys of D and A.   y Pivot chord between keys of A and D

5. (*a*) Avoid having two forms of the same chord, either minor or major, with only one or two other chords between them.

(*b*) A note in one chord should not be followed by the same note chromatically altered in another key, except when the root of the 2nd chord is the 3rd of the 1st chord, or if the second note is the 7th of the dominant 7th.

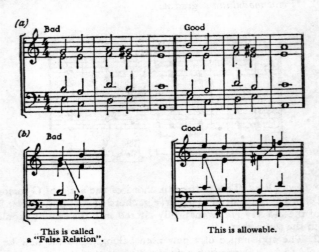

This is called a "False Relation".

This is allowable.

6. *Transition.* This is abrupt modulation dispensing with the pivot chord. A chord belonging to the old key is immediately followed by a chord from the new key, each having a note in common and generally a chromatic movement in one of the parts, e.g.

7. *Table of modulation to nearly related keys*

C major to relative A minor	. . .	{ F major, D minor,
A minor to relative C major	. . .	B diminished
C major to dominant G major	. . .	A minor, E minor
A minor to dominant E minor	. . .	A minor
C major to subdominant F major	. . .	A minor, D minor
A minor to subdominant D minor	. . .	D minor

C major to supertonic D minor	.	.	.	D minor
C major to mediant E minor	.	.	.	A minor
A minor to relative major of dominant G major	.			A minor
A minor to relative major of subdominant F major	.			D minor

8. Modulations should not be effected too soon. The tonic key should be established firmly first.

9. Modulating sequences, in different keys, commonly occur after a central cadence.

Bach.: Prelude No. 2, Book II. *Forty eight Preludes and Fugues*

The above excerpt from Bach gives sequences in alternate diatonic 7ths and 9ths. The following is a sequence from Debussy:

Debussy: 'Doctor Gradus ad Parnassum' from 'Children's Corner' suite

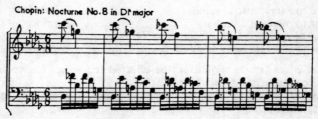

Chopin: Nocturne No. 8 in D♭ major

Note the harmonies are built over the pedal note of D♭.

Two further useful chords are: the Neapolitan 6th, which is one of the chromatic chords. It is the major common chord on the flattened supertonic, in its first inversion, ie. in C major, F, A♭ and D♭; the German form of the Augmented Sixth, ie. in C major, A♭, C, E♭ and F♯. By enharmonic change of the F♯-G♭ can become a dominant 7th.

CHAPTER SEVEN

Form in Music

THE STUDENT HAS BY NOW probably learnt quite a lot about music—time, melodic writing, harmony, keys, expression marks and signs—and he has probably read a lot of musical history and listened to a great deal of music. It is to be hoped that his ears have been trained to recognize what he hears and his eyes to visualize melodies and cadences.

But he must also be able to understand the architectural way, or 'form', in which music is built up if he is to reap full enjoyment from his studies, quite apart from 'cramming' sufficient knowledge to pass an examination.

Rhythm has always been a strong factor in the lives of men. Up to the sixteenth century music was unbarred, although in the music of Palestrina, for instance, the harmony can be heard to move towards definite rhythmical points. This occurs in spite of the fact that the modes employed did not use the cadence points which became familiar in later times.

In the seventeenth and eighteenth centuries music became much more ordered in character. Forms became very rigid and stereotyped in order to please the ears of the nobility, who provided the audiences for most of the music composed.

Dance forms of various kinds formed the basis for composition, and these were later formed into suites. See chapter of Some General Definitions for details of these early dance forms, as well as the more developed ones arising in a later age, when men sought for freer styles to express the new concepts of liberty and individualism, which arose with the revolutionary tide at the end of the eighteenth century.

After the French Revolution and its ideas of liberty, equality and fraternity, this rigidity was relaxed and the rise of romanticism in art and literature was also reflected in the breaking of the harmonic rules of the past as well as the introduction of all sorts of structural irregularities into musical forms (see remarks on phrasing, below).

In a still later age, at the turn of the present century, men felt obliged to turn to even stranger forms to express disillusion with middle-class society, bewilderment and escapism. Impressionism in music tended to attempt the portrayal of such things as water sounds and not feelings, atonality could be appreciated on paper if not always in the concert-room and ordinary people turned to musical plays and jazz in order to find tunes and rhythms which they could understand.

In order, then, to understand the structure of great music, the basic and fundamental elements have to be examined and analysed in a detailed way. The following chapters show the build-up of structure as well as departures from the rule and should be very carefully studied. The listed works should also be played and analysed by the student with the guidance of the teacher. A great deal of Beethoven has been put forward as examples because most people possess or can obtain Beethoven sonatas very easily from public libraries. Also, Beethoven's music shows the points to be considered in such a great and wonderful way that it is worth much study.

Orchestral music is also put forward as examples because much of this appears in the set works of examination papers.

Apart from this, many easy pieces are quoted which even a pianist at a very elementary stage can play.

ACCENT

A great deal has probably been learnt about accent from the chapters on time and rhythm, and rhythmic and melodic aural tests, but for the sake of clarity the student should understand that music has come to be written in definite rhythms of various kinds with accented or stronger notes as an indication of the time groupings employed, e.g.

Two beats in a bar, or duple time.

Three beats in a bar, or triple time.
(See table of time signatures in chapter on time.)

These accented notes are also organized into stronger and weaker notes or bars. Look at this excerpt from the song, 'Whither', by Schubert:

Play this song from the original copy and you will see that the strong beat, or place where the arrow points, is a cadence. (See the chapter on cadences in four-part harmony.)

There are other kinds of groupings, although these tend to be more rare. The following from the Scherzo in Beethoven's Ninth Symphony will illustrate this:

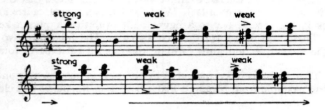

Remember, imperfect and interrupted cadences are temporary resting points and perfect and the rarer plagal cadences are final resting-points.

FIGURES

These are small groupings of notes, repeated quite often throughout a composition and helping to form a unity of style over a basic idea:

Schumann, Symphony no. 4 in D minor

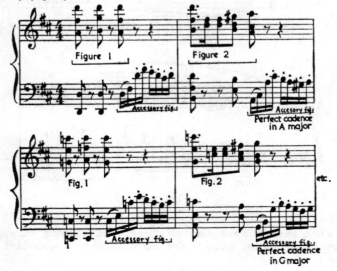

Many other figures occur in great music, and the student is urged to find as many as possible for himself. Some pieces are made up almost entirely of repeated figures, such as Chopin's Etude in C# minor.

SECTIONS, PHRASES AND SENTENCES

If you look at the last example again you will notice that the first figure is built over the chords I, IV, I (which is a plagal cadence) and resolves in the second bar to a figure built over the dominant key, A major. These two bars form the first SECTION. The following two bars form the second section, thus forming the most usual type of four-bar phrase.

The phrase is often indicated by the phrase mark or slur and the following example from Mozart's Piano Sonata in B♭ shows this clearly:

The above example forms the first phrase. The following example is the answering phrase, which is also one which cannot be divided into sections:

Undivided phrase

etc,

This is also called the responsive phrase.

These two phrases form the common type of musical SENTENCE.

Romantic composers often broke the rule regarding continuation of movement beyond cadence points. See, for example, Liszt's 'Liebestraum' and Schubert's Piano Sonata in A, op. 120.

Some sentences have three phrases: see Chopin's Mazurka in B♭, op. 7, bars 1-4, announcing phrase; bars 5-8, first responsive phrase; bars 9-12, second responsive phrase. See also Brahms's Waltz, op. 39, and Grieg's, *Albumblätter*, op. 28, the first part of 'Rule Britannia', the opening of the Minuet of Beethoven's Pianoforte Sonata in F minor, op. 2, no. 1, the first movement of the same composer's Sonata in F major, op. 10, no. 2, also the opening of the Scherzo of Schumann's Symphony in C major.

For four-phrase sentences see Mozart's *Don Giovanni* and the aria 'Dalla sua pace'. See also Chopin's Prelude, op. 28, no. 17.

EXTENSIONS OF PHRASES

In order to maintain interest and avoid squareness, composers have developed the habit of extending or contracting phrases. The following is an extension in which *the cadence chord is prolonged or augmented*:

Mendelssohn, Lobgesang

Some *cadences* are *repeated or postponed*, as in the following example:

Beethoven, Pianoforte Sonata in A♭, op. 26

At 'X' the cadence of C minor replaces the expected one of E♭ major, which actually occurs two bars later, thus prolonging the phrase to six bars.

Interpolation. This is the insertion of a new bar in the midst of a phrase or the restatement of a bar or bars either exactly, or slightly, altered:

Mozart, Sonata in F, no. 1, K.533

Contraction of phrases. This is done by starting one phrase on the last note of another, e.g. overlapping or shortening:

Mendelssohn, no. 11 of *Songs without Words*

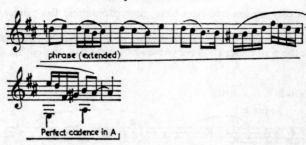

BINARY OR TWO-PART FORM

Simple Binary form is well illustrated in the following song:

'The Bailiff's Daughter of Islington'

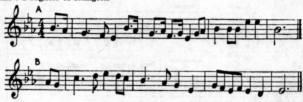

Here the music naturally divides itself into two equal parts, A and B, the second part being the response to the first.

Binary form is constantly met with in hymn-tunes, folk-songs and dance movements by reason of its exactitude, lending itself readily to the writings of seventeenth- and eighteenth-century composers. It usually modulates from the tonal centre (tonic) to the dominant in the middle of the piece, and then reverts to tonic for the finish. See especially a gavotte from the *6th French Suite*, by J. S. Bach, and the Andante Cantabile of Mozart's Pianoforte Sonata in C, which contains two melodies, each in binary form. Beethoven has immortalized this form in the Andante from his Pianoforte Sonata in F minor, op. 57, the first eight bars being repeated and forming part A and the second eight bars, also repeated, forming part B. See also 'Modulation' in Chapters 4 and 6.

Although this form is still used today for short, simple pieces and variations, in the course of time it was somewhat altered by composers, who took to repeating the first four bars at the end of the second part, thus leading to a form which lent itself more readily to variety.

TERNARY FORM

This is mainly used in the building up of sonatas, symphonies and overtures.

Look at 'The Blue Bells of Scotland'.

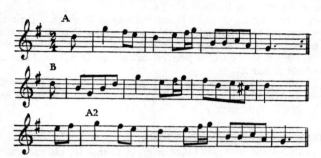

A. Statement.
B. Digression (or development).
A2. Restatement (or recapitulation).

Ternary form can be found in many folk-songs and is obviously a natural expression for melody with variety in its middle part. In the hands of great composers, it developed into countless variable forms of great beauty and diversity. A classical example is the Menuetto from Mozart's Symphony in C major, and amongst the Romantics one can take the Valse Allemande from Schumann's *Carnaval*.

Sometimes the parts are held together by linking passages, as the little Romance from Beethoven's Sonatina in G major. In other works the parts are woven imperceptibly together by subtle key changes, as in the Allegretto from Beethoven's Pianoforte Sonata in F minor, op. 2, no. 1.

The coda. Later an extension of the original idea was placed at the end of the piece and called the CODA (see First Movement Form).

Extensions were also added to the form, and the following work by Mendelssohn should be very carefully studied in its original to give an idea of the inherent variety obtainable in ternary form. The two introductory bars are given below as a guide:

Allegro con fuoco, no. 26 from *Songs without Words*

A. The theme begins in tonic at the second half of bar 3, with a half cadence at bar 7. A sequential extension occurs at bars 10 and 11, and a second extension of phrase by cadential interruption ends the division in a perfect cadence at bar 14.

B. This begins at bar 15 and modulates through G minor and C minor (bar 16) to G minor (bar 18) and D minor (bar 20). A cadential interruption begins at the end of bar 22, and is followed by an extension of sentence by repetition to a perfect cadence in D minor, finishing on the first beat of bar 25.

A linking passage over a pedal note of D leads to a modulatory passage at bar 28 which lasts until the theme A2 is reached in the middle of bar 29 in the tonic key.

THE MINUET and MINUET AND TRIO FORM

At this point attention must be given to that simple and charming dance form, the minuet, in $\frac{3}{4}$ time, because sonata first movement form grew from it, as well as the symphony and the overture

The minuet was originally a sixteenth-century French dance, sometimes in binary but usually in ternary form. Many minuets were written for the European courts, and to avoid monotony they came to be written in pairs. The second one was called a 'trio', because it was played by three instruments. It became the custom to play the first minuet through twice with repeats. The trio, often written in a relative minor key, was then played twice with repeats, and the minuet was then played again without repeats.

Many beautiful minuets and trios have been written, two well-known ones being the one by Boccherini and the little one in G by Beethoven.

At first they were rather square, beginning on the first beat of the bar, but Haydn wrote them commencing on the third beat of the bar, thereby increasing the elasticity of the form. They also came to be played slightly faster than before.

The young pianist should play the Minuet and Trio in C by Haydn (Grade III Standard, Associated Board) to obtain a good idea of this form, but so many thousands of others have been written that he should have no difficulty in finding plenty of material to examine.

In his symphonies Haydn also provided linking passages between the minuets and trios in order to keep up the movement and avoid squareness of design.

Later composers took the minuet and trio form as a basis for other dances, such as polaccas, polonaises, mazurkas, etc. Grieg has used both binary and ternary form for his 'Rigaudon' in the Pianoforte Suite, 'Aus Holberg's Zeit'.

THE SCHERZO

Beethoven developed the already quickened minuet into the scherzo, his own scherzos becoming increasingly faster, such as the one beat in a bar movement of the Scherzo of the Ninth Symphony (see first example on page 75).

Nineteenth-century composers also composed scherzos as pieces of a light character to be performed alone or in a suite. Mendelssohn's scherzos are usually in sonata form.

THE EPISODE

The Trio, contrasted in character, developed into the episode, which is a complete theme appearing only once in a movement. It is much more developed than the middle part of a ternary section which is simply the development of the main idea in other keys.

Minuet and trio form has also been taken for lyrical pieces, such as nocturnes, impromptus and romances, as well as slow movements of symphonies and sonatas. The clearest example of this is in the slow movement from Beethoven's Sonata in G for pianoforte, op. 79. The movements in this case are in binary form, the first diversion finishing in the tonic key in bar 8. There is a linking passage to the episode beginning in E♭ in bar 10. This modulates back to tonic in bar 21. The original theme is then played exactly as at the beginning, and the whole finished with a coda at bars 30 to 34.

Note: The minuet and trio form is, of course, an extended kind of ternary form.

THE RONDO

This probably grew up from songs in which one person sang solo verses and others joined in with the refrain.

The musical rondo or old rondo form is usually built up as follows:

A.   Theme in binary form.
B.   Episode 1, also in binary form.
A2. Theme repeated.
C.   Episode 2, also in binary form.
A3. Theme repeated.
Coda.

At first amongst the early French composers the episodes did not vary much from the original theme (see Francois Couperin, Rondo, *La Tendre Fanchon*).

However, as the rondo was developed by such composers as Haydn and Mozart, the episodes became much clearer in form and appeared in other related keys. All sections were also often ternary in form. A very beautiful example is the last movement of Mozart's great C minor Sonata, K.457.

Beethoven's 'Vivace' from the Sonata in G major, op. 79, is also another very beautiful example of the older rondo:

A.   Bars 1 to 16, repeated, in G major.

Link of two bars.
B. First episode in E minor, bars 18 to 24.
    Link or transition founded on figure of principal theme,
    bars 24 to 34.
A2. Principle theme repeated in tonic, bars 35 to 50.
C. Second episode with ornamented repetition of a single
    sentence, bars 50 to 66.
    Linking passage bars 67 to 71.
A3. Variation on principal theme, bars 72 to 95.
Coda, also founded on principal theme, bars 96 to end.

The *sonata rondo* is much less square and rigid than the old rondo.
One part leads into the other without a break. It is made up as follows:

A. Principal subject in tonic.
B. Second subject, usually in dominant.
A2. Principal subject again in tonic.
C. Episode in another related key.
A3. Principal subject a third time in tonic.
B2. Second subject once more in tonic,
A4. Final appearance of principal subject.

or

A coda which is mainly composed of the principal subject.

See the very beautiful last movement rondo by Beethoven in the Sonata,
op. 2, no. 2. It gives a very clear picture of Sonata Rondo.

SONATA FORM

(The 17th century meaning of the word 'sonata' was a composition played on an instrument, as against a piece which was sung, i.e. a
'cantata'.)

The earliest forms of sonatas were written in Italy and were in
binary form (see the sonatas of Scarlatti). The A section was in tonic,
modulating to dominant, and in section B the dominant modulated back
to tonic.

It was the suite, or collection of dances, contrasted in character
and key, which led towards the sonata or 'cyclic work'.

The pianoforte sonata from Haydn's time onwards is usually of
three movements. The most common arrangement of movements is:

First movement. Moderato. See following section on first movement
    form.
Slow movement. Adagio. Sometimes in minuet and trio form.
Finale. Sonata rondo, old rondo or an allegro movement of first move-
    ment form,

or

Theme and variations.

When a sonata is written for more than two instruments it is called a—

> Trio: 3 instruments.
> Quartet: 4 instruments.
> Quintet: 5 instruments.
> Sextet: 6 instruments.
> Septet: 7 instruments.
> Octet: 8 instruments.

Haydn did very much to develop the string quartet, partly because some of his noble supporters played instruments themselves.

A sonata for orchestra is called a SYMPHONY. Symphonies and quartets are usually in four movements—that is, a minuet and trio or scherzo is inserted between the slow movement and the finale.

The movements of these sonatas or symphonies are usually written in contrasting keys. The first and last movements are mostly in tonic and the slow movement in a nearly related key—in older works dominant or relative minor.

In later compositions other and remoter keys are used.

Sometimes sonatas and symphonies have fewer or more movements. Several of Mozart's violin and piano sonatas are in two movements, as well as Beethoven's Piano Sonatas, op. 49, 54, 78, 90 and 111. These are nearly all written in tonic, although sometimes one movement is in minor and the other in major. Some symphonies, such as Schumann's no. 3 in E♭ are in five movements, the additional movement being in some key closely related to the whole work.

Some more recent writers retain the classical form, but Bruckner, for instance, is inclined to have alternately fast and slow themes within one movement. Some symphonies reverse the order of the movements. Tchaikovsky's 'Pathetic' Symphony, for instance, ends with a slow movement, adagio lamentoso.

FIRST MOVEMENT FORM

We have already said that early sonatas were written in binary or two-part form.

Seventeenth-century composers developed the cadence figure at the end of each part until it nearly assumed the character of a second subject:

From Sonata in D, no. 10, by Domenico Paradies (1710-92)

Here is the developed cadential material:

and the design became:

A	**B**
(a) First theme in tonic, modulating to	(a) Opening theme in dominant with some expansion, modulating to
(b) Second theme often in dominant.	(b) Second theme in tonic.

Later on the opening theme in dominant in the second section was often followed immediately by a restatement of the same theme in tonic, just before the second theme in tonic.

C. P. E. Bach, son of the great Johann Sebastian, was very inventive, and whilst his music is rather dull, later composers came to model much of their work on his experiments.

The final design of the first movement form became the form in which we know it today, by the inclusion of the development.

A. *Exposition*
    First subject in tonic key.
        Transition or bridge to
    Second subject in dominant or another related key.
    Codetta ending at double bar in dominant.
    This is repeated.
B. The *development*, which is a free fantasia through several keys leading to

A2. *Recapitulation.* The first and second subjects are repeated in tonic and end in a coda, also in tonic.

This was the design employed by the great masters, Haydn, Mozart and Beethoven, and developed by them to its greatest depths of expression.

INTRODUCTION

This comes at the beginning of a symphony or sonata, and is supposed to condition the minds of the audience to the music to follow. Sometimes it consists of two chords, such as in Beethoven's Third Symphony, or it is quite long, as in his Seventh Symphony. It is usually slow.

THE EXPOSITION

This usually contains all the main musical ideas of the piece. It begins with the *subject*. This consists mostly of some pithy material, which the listener can remember, such as in the famous Fifth Symphony by Beethoven:

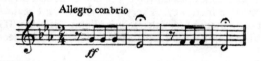

Other examples from great music are Mozart's Pianoforte Sonata in C minor, Beethoven's Pianoforte Sonata in A, op. 2, no. 2, Schumann's Symphony in C, Grieg's Sonata in C minor for pianoforte and violin, Dvořák's 'New World' Symphony and Smetana's String Quartet in E minor.

The first subject is in tonic. It may modulate a little, but the key 'centre' or the part of longest duration is tonic. The subject is not very long—only one or two sentences—and often ends with a perfect or half-cadence.

The first subject may consist of several ideas and is sometimes called a 'first subject group'.

THE TRANSITION, BRIDGE PASSAGE OR LINK

This is much less definite in character than the first subject. Eighteenth-century audiences were not very accustomed to the new first movement sonata form, and the transition was then mostly composed of broken chords and scales. Even Mozart had to bow to the demands of the

period and write a transition passage like this in his Sonata in B♭ major
K.570, bars 21 and 22—

before the second subject begins at bar 23.

As people became more used to the sonata form, they did not need
such obvious signposts to tell them where they were in music, and it
became possible to write transition passages that were things of great
beauty in themselves and welded into the whole so as to make the entire
movement one living thing.

Sometimes the transition is composed entirely of new matter, such
as in Beethoven's Pianoforte Sonata, op. 31, no. 2, where it begins in
tonic at bar 21 and continues until bar 41, where the second subject enters
in A minor, the dominant key. A very well-known and beautiful example
is in the first movement of Mendelssohn's Violin Concerto. It commences
at bar 72 and continues right up to bar 131, where the second subject
begins.

At other times the transition is a continuation of the same thematic
material, such as in the third and last movement of the 'Moonlight'
Sonata, op. 27, no. 2, by Beethoven. Here the transition begins at bar 15
and consists of the same kind of broken chords as the first subject. The
second subject begins at bar 21.

Sometimes, again, the transition consists of new thematic material
as well as material from the first subject. See the first movement of Beethoven's Pianoforte Sonata, op. 31, no. 3. The transition begins in bar 25
and consists of fresh material as well as the original motive. It ends at
bar 45 with the beginning of the second subject.

How to find the Beginning of the Transition. Quite often the first
subject finishes with a perfect cadence in the tonic key, although as in
Mozart's Sonata in D, no. 10, this occurs at bar 9 and is followed by a
half-cadence in tonic at bar 17.

Another possibility is to look at the *Recapitulation* (*q.v.*). Here the
first and second subjects are often repeated in another key and the
transition is different from the one in the beginning.

Finally, it should be noted that form itself serves only as a basis
or guide for composition, and great composers have shown their skill by
creating diverse and beautiful music from several modest themes, not

adhering rigidly to structural rules, but making gradual movements from one subject to another.

THE SECOND SUBJECT

This is usually a contrast to the first subject, but similar in style so that it fits well with the whole movement. There may be several subjects, called first section, second section, third section, etc. (See the Pianoforte Sonata of Beethoven in F major, op. 10, no. 2.)

Section 1 of the second subject begins at bar 18.
Section 2 begins at bar 38.
Section 3 begins at bar 47.
Section 4 begins at bar 55.

Until Beethoven's time the second subject was written in dominant if the tonic key was major and relative major if the tonic key was minor. Beethoven, however, varied the kinds of keys used, choosing such contrasts as the mediant major, the submediant major and the dominant minor. Sometimes the second subject begins in one key and continues in another. It still depends entirely on the skill of the composer as to how beautiful he can make a work sound, whatever key he uses.

Here is a small excerpt from Beethoven's Pianoforte Sonata in G major, op. 79, first movement, which may be familiar to young students. The second subject begins—

 *etc.*

in bar 24 in A major and modulates later to D major in which key it ends.

Notice that in the recapitulation the same key relationship continues. The same theme begins at bar 146 in D major and modulates, as before, to a key a 5th below, e.g. G major, the tonic key. This procedure is fairly general.

THE CODETTA

This is the last section of the exposition and was originally some sort of embroidered cadence. In Mozart's 'Jupiter' Symphony (K.551), for instance, the second subject ends with repeated cadences. Beethoven, however, changed all this until it ceased being mere 'padding', but became an artistic creation in its own right. See his Pianoforte Sonata in E minor, op. 90.

After the codetta the exposition comes to an end with a double bar and a repeat. This is often dispensed with nowadays, especially in an emotional work, where it may upset the feeling for the climax of the work. However, in former times it was considered part of the whole design, and often had a passage linking back to the beginning. See Mozart's Pianoforte Sonata in C minor (K.457).

THE DEVELOPMENT

This can be compared with that part of a novel or play where, after all the characters have been introduced, they begin to show signs of peculiar or individual behaviour.

Here the composer can use one or any of the themes from the exposition and improvise upon them in any way he may wish. This may have developed from the old custom of a performing musician showing how brilliant he was at inventing variations over melodies in public and on the spur of the moment.

The various ways of making such a free fantasia are as follows:

1. *Change of Key or Tonality.* This is the idea in the exposition:

Beethoven's Pianoforte Sonata in A major, no. 2

This is the opening of the development:

This comes later in the development:

2. *Change of Accompaniment and Change of Register.* This is also shown in the example above.

3. *Varied Harmonization.* Look at the following example from

Brahms's Sonata for pianoforte and violin in G major, op. 78.

4. *Variety of Rhythmic Treatment.* Listen to Schumann's Pianoforte Concerto in A minor:

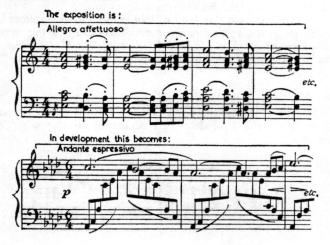

Listen, also, to Beethoven's Symphony in F, no. 8, and notice how the opening of the first subject is altered in the development by extending the phrase lengths.

5. *Contrapuntal Treatment.* See Mozart's famous Symphony in G minor (K.550). The first subject is developed later. Firstly, the melody is put into the bass and a contrapuntal part added above. Then the melody is put into the treble and a similar counterpart put in the bass.

6. *Figures may be Worked Up.* Notice that the counterpoint in the development section of Mozart's G minor Symphony quoted above is based on the accompanying figure in the first subject.

7. *Phrases may be Augmented or Diminished,* such as in Dvořák's 'New World' Symphony:

In all this it should be noted that the tonic key is generally avoided in order to leave it fresh to return to in the recapitulation, and that modulation is used as much as is artistically possible.

Wagner has used this kind of free fantasia to great effect in his music dramas by taking his themes or leitmotives and weaving them into extraordinary effects. *Tristan und Isolde* and *Die Meistersinger* offer wonderful examples of this kind of treatment.

THE EPISODE

Sometimes during the development a fresh theme is introduced which is called the 'episode'. This occurs in Beethoven's 'Eroica' Symphony—

and Mendelssohn's 'Italian' Symphony:

Examples also occur in Beethoven's Pianoforte Sonatas, op. 10, no. 2, and op. 41, no. 1, and in Mozart's Pianoforte and Violin Sonata in E♭, no. 7.

The Approach to the Recapitulation. During the fantasia the key moves gradually towards the tonic, but in the eighteenth century the usual custom was to end the development section firmly on the dominant (see Haydn's Symphony in E♭, no. 1, and Mozart's Pianoforte Sonata in B♭ (K.333). The following excerpt from Mozart's Symphony in G minor shows how beautiful this sort of treatment can become:

Another different but beautiful example is in Beethoven's Pianoforte Sonata, op. 53.

Later writers allow the music to flow more continuously from the development into the recapitulation. See, for instance, Mendelssohn's Symphony in A, no. 4, and Tchaikovsky's Fifth Symphony in E minor, also Brahms's Symphony in C minor.

THE RECAPITULATION

Up to now we have studied the A and B sections of the ternary form. Now we come to A2, or the return, which is done in a very similar way to the return of the minuet in the minuet and trio form.

The whole exposition is usually repeated, except that the second subject is repeated in tonic, and the transition is therefore modified. Compare the transition in the exposition in Beethoven's Pianoforte Sonata in E♭, op. 31, no. 3, with that of the recapitulation. You will see that the second transition is considerably shorter than the first.

Sometimes the transition is left out altogether. Brahms has done this in his Sonata for violin and piano in G, op. 78.

If the second subject is in a remote key, such as the mediant, it usually also appears in the recapitulation in a remote key, working gradually towards tonic. However, in the works of nineteenth-century composers the tendency is to either treat the themes in the recapitulation in a different way, to alter the keys, or to introduce the main themes in a different order.

THE CODA

Sometimes a piece may be complete at the end of the recapitulation, but usually a coda is added. This is very rarely of new material, and in some cases has been so broadened out as almost to form a fourth section of the movement. Beethoven especially has very lovely codas in his piano sonatas, and the student should make every effort to listen to them. They are: op. 2, no. 3; op. 7; op. 27, no. 2, last movement; op. 31, no. 3; op. 53; op. 57; op. 81A, op. 90; op. 106 and op. 111.

VARIATION FORM

This is a very old form. It is generally built over an original theme in binary or two-part form, which, if you remember, is composed of two sentences of two four-bar phrases (see binary form).

Composers have always felt the need for music which continually leads the interest forward, but in the early days of instrumental composition they lacked the form with which to achieve this effect. Therefore the theme was constantly changed in repetition in order to achieve variety. See, for instance, 'The Carman's Whistle', by William Byrd, and notice the sort of variations composers were making in the sixteenth century. Right through the seventeenth and eighteenth centuries dance music was embellished in this way, and one is forced to think of Mr. Louis Armstrong and the way he and his friends improvise upon a dance-tune theme at a jam session.

If you take the 'Courante avec deux Doubles' from *Suite Anglaise* in A major, by J. S. Bach, you will see that it is a courante with two variations. In spite of the richer style used, the idea is the same as in 'The Carman's Whistle'.

Up to and including Bach's time, the ground-bass, or 'basso ostinato'—that is, a constantly recurring bass theme—has been used as a kind of variation. See the ground-bass in Purcell's *Dido and Aeneas* and the same composer's well-known Air on a ground-bass commencing thus:

But, of course, a far greater one is in Bach's great B minor Mass. It is the 'Crucifixus', founded upon the following 'ground':

This is repeated twelve times, and many beautiful harmonies are built over it.

Haydn wrote many variations, but Mozart's on the theme of 'Ah, vous dirai-je, Maman' (K.265) give delight both to the young student and the virtuoso concert pianist, who can find therein great opportunities to show off his sparkling technique.

Beethoven wrote many great and wonderful variations, including those for piano on a theme of Diabelli. This theme has thirty-three variations, which go through almost all keys with much richness and diversity of melody and rhythm. Perhaps the greatest peak of all is reached in the variations of the Pianoforte Sonata, op. 111, where Beethoven's music almost seems to touch the fringes of another world.

Of the later composers, Schumann has written a major work, the *Etudes Symphoniques*, also for piano. Brahms has written many variations, including Variations and Fugue on a Theme by Handel for piano, op. 24, and a set for orchestra in B♭ on a theme by Haydn, op. 56A. The famous 'Enigma' Variations by Elgar are an example of modern treatment of this form.

Variations are composed in many different ways, such as the following:

1. The theme altered by a change of tempo. See Grieg's allegro furioso from Ballade in G minor, op. 24.

2. Theme differently harmonized, the melody little altered, if at all. See Variation 1 of *Seventeen Variations Sérieuses* by Mendelssohn op. 54.

3. Ornamentation or figuration of theme. See Mozart's 'Ah, vous dirai-je, Maman' (K.265), Variations 2, 4, 5, 9 and 10.

4. Melody changed, harmonic basis kept. See Variation 9 from Beethoven's Thirty-two Variations in C minor.

5. Only a slight connection retained of the original theme, usually rhythmical. See Variations on a Theme of Haydn, by Brahms, and Beethoven's 'Diabelli' Variations.

6. Contrapuntal treatment, e.g. canon or fugue. See Beethoven's Fifteen Variations on a Theme from the 'Eroica', Variation 7, 'Canone all' ottava' and the 'Finale alla fuga'.

For CADENZA, CONCERTO, FUGUE, OVERTURE, SUITE and SYMPHONY see Chapter 14.

CHAPTER EIGHT

Musical Signs

EXPRESSION MARKS

f = forte = loud.	*mp* = mezzo-piano = half soft.
mf = mezzo-forte = half loud.	*p* = piano = soft.
ff = double forte = very loud.	*pp* = double piano = very soft.
fff = treble forte = as loud as possible.	*ppp* = treble piano = as soft as possible.

——————————————— = crescendo = gradually becoming louder.

——————————————— = diminuendo = gradually becoming softer.

sf, fz, sfz = sforzando = play note or chord at which it is placed louder.

fp = forte-piano = play note or chord at which it is placed loud and the very next notes softly.

VARIOUS USES OF CURVED LINES

The TIE The second note is held, but not played if no other note is between.

The SLUR All notes to be played smoothly or legato. For stringed instruments, it means notes to be played with one bow.

The PHRASE MARK

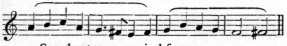

See chapter on musical form.

The PORTAMENTO  For singers, this means carrying the voice from one note to the next with no break in the sound.

For ev - er more

The GLISSANDO  This means the same as portamento, but is used for stringed instruments or piano.

STACCATO SIGNS

Mezzo staccato — notes shortened by one quarter

Staccato notes — shortened by a half

Staccatissimo — notes shortened by three-quarters

played

SIGNS OF ACCENTUATION

 *plus staccato

PAUSE MARKS

= G.P. = general pause. If this is over a note, the note is usually held for half its value again.

L.P. = lunga pause = long pause.
, = slight pause or, for singers, a breath-mark.

SIGNS OF PITCH

8*va*
or 8 } = play passage an octave higher than written.
8*va* bassa or 8*va* sotto = play an octave lower than written.

STRINGED INSTRUMENT SIGNS

⊓ ⊔ = down bow.   V = an up bow.

ORCHESTRAL INSTRUMENTS

Zu 2 = two instruments to play the same part.

CHANGE OF KEY

C major   C minor   D major

PIANOFORTE SIGNS

The Spread Chord. To be played from the bottom upwards, holding each note down after it is played. In music from before the eighteenth century it may be played from the top down.

Pedal Marks

U.C. =una corda =put down soft pedal.

T.C. =tre corde =raise soft pedal.

.... or Ped. ————* or |_____| =put down sustaining pedal at the first sign; continue along the line and raise at the second sign.

L.H. =left hand.

R.H. =right hand.

D.S. =dal segno =go back to the sign.

D.C. =da capo =go back to the beginning.

M.S. =mano sinistra =left hand.

M.D. =mano destra =right hand.

M.G. =main gauche =left hand.

M.D. =main droite =right hand.

Metronome Marks, such as MM ♩ =100. Invented by Loulié in 1696, the pyramid-shaped one now in use was invented by Maelzel (1772-1838). He was a friend of Beethoven, who used it for his compositions.

The metronome can be set to the speed required, such as the one above, which means that each crotchet is to be played at the speed ticked out when the metronome is set at 100, or 100 crotchets per minute.

Metronome speeds, even when set by composers, should only be used as a guide and not rigidly adhered to, as the speed suitable for one type of performer is not always suitable for another, and even great composers may be at fault in their markings. Also, a performance which properly carries out all the accents and expression marks indicated in a composition can sound as fast as a speedier one without them.

Repeat Marks

The double bar 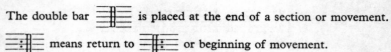 is placed at the end of a section or movement.

means return to or beginning of movement.

 etc.

This means play to bar 1 and then repeat the passage, but play bar 2 instead of bar 1 the second time through.

Orchestral Repeat Marks

CHAPTER NINE

Ornaments

ORNAMENTS, THE MUSICAL MEANING of which is 'melodic decoration', generally came into use in order to give more meaning and colour to a melodic line. As the tone of many instruments played in the past was colourless and dull, decoration of a melody greatly added to the diversity and interest of the playing.

The earliest recorded vocal shake or trill is from the third century. Italian singers decorated plainsong before the tenth century, and although this practice was decried from time to time by Church authorities, it continued to flourish even when music became polyphonic. A composer often wrote the bare notes only and the performer—singer, lute-player or organist—ornamented the music, as in the following example by Palestrina:

Hymn-tunes have often been embellished by congregations, and the Spaniard of today still embroiders simple tunes when he sings them.

However, the heyday of embellishment of melodies was in the seventeenth and eighteenth centuries and much music by great composers, such as Handel and Purcell, was elaborately ornamented by the singers of their time. Lutenists and harpsichordists also availed themselves of the current practice because of the lack of sustaining power of their instruments.

Ornaments or Melodic Decoration

The ornaments used were many and varied and most of them have dropped out of use. The main ones employed today are listed hereunder but arguments regarding interpretation still exist around the playing of ornaments of the sixteenth- and seventeenth-century composers. In a later era Chopin, for instance, sometimes changed the ornamentation of his own compositions with every performance.

An attempt is made here to indicate clearly definitions acceptable to examination authorities, whilst at the same time giving the student some idea of possible readings in actual performance.

THE ACCIACCATURA

 with a stroke through the first note. Written out

as: 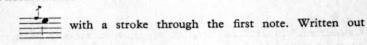 This is accepted by examiners.

The acciaccatura is played in this way in music by early composers of the sixteenth and seventeenth centuries as well as thus

or thus The precise duration of the notes cannot always be determined in modern editions, owing to lack of clarity of the real purpose of the composer, and the context has to decide the issue.

The remarks apply equally to the *double appoggiatura*

and the *triple appoggiatura*

The acciaccatura with the spread chord, sometimes

performed thus: with the final note on the beat, but in

early music always thus: with the *first* note played on the beat.

THE TURN

 is performed thus: or thus:

according to taste and context. In Wagner it is performed thus in many instances: . On the beat it is performed thus: 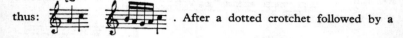. After a dotted crotchet followed by a

quaver it is performed thus: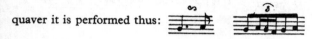

THE INVERTED TURN

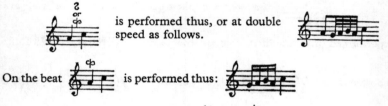

is performed thus, or at double speed as follows.

On the beat is performed thus:

The turn with accidental: . The same principles

apply as for the mordent with accidentals.

THE TRILL OR SHAKE

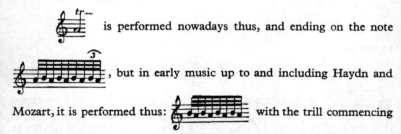

is performed nowadays thus, and ending on the note

, but in early music up to and including Haydn and

Mozart, it is performed thus: with the trill commencing

on the upper note according to context. Bach trills are often played at a slower rate in slow movements. In Haydn or Mozart the performer uses his own discretion as whether or not to trill from the note above the written note, although usually the trill begins from the upper note.

The modern composer will clearly indicate his intentions, e.g.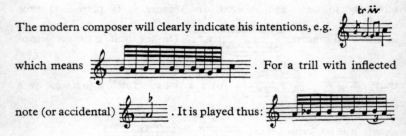

which means   . For a trill with inflected

note (or accidental)   . It is played thus:

THE APPOGGIATURA

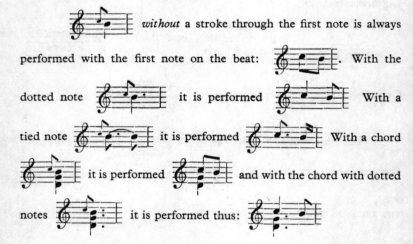

    without a stroke through the first note is always

performed with the first note on the beat: . With the

dotted note   it is performed   With a

tied note   it is performed   With a chord

    it is performed   and with the chord with dotted

notes   it is performed thus:

MORDENTS

    The upper mordent   is often performed thus:

    with the grace notes coming before the beat. In early music

it is often played thus: but research into ornaments as

played in Bach's time reveals that it was played thus: ,

commencing on the note above the first note indicated as well as on the beat.

The upper mordent with accidental is performed

thus: or in any other of the ways mentioned above, according

to the type of music performed.

The lower mordent . This is mostly encountered only in

early music and is performed thus: or thus:

with the first note falling on the beat.

The lower mordent with accidental is performed

thus: or at half-speed as above.

CHAPTER TEN

Keyboard Instruments

IT WAS, of course, the Greek, Pythagoras, who discovered the numerical relationship of notes, by means of the number of vibrations needed to produce different sounds. He showed how to split the octave into two tetrachords (see page 19), and is said to have been responsible for the Greek system of musical notation.

Demonstrating his principles, which are used today in the modern piano, he also invented an instrument called the MONOCHORD. 'This consisted of one string which was divided into sections to show how different notes could be produced on it. By dividing the string exactly in half, a note an octave higher could be sounded. The same note could be made by a string vibrating at twice the speed. Two-thirds of the string would make a note a 5th higher and all the other notes had mathematical proportions. The first five harmonics of low C are thus forming the common chord. The 6th harmonic is B♭ which makes the chord known as the dominant 7th.'* You can find some of the harmonics on the piano. If you play the G below middle C so slowly that it does not sound and then play the C below loudly, the G will sound above middle C. Because of equal temperament, however, some of the other harmonics cannot be found on the modern piano.

A performing version of the monochord is called the tromba marina, and was still used in the days of the young Mozart. Another development of the monochord is the Norwegian landleik. Other nearly related instruments are the zither, cittern, dulcimer, psaltery, opharion, bandore, pandore and the bandurria and laud, which are still popular in Spain today.

Our present finger keyboard came into use in the thirteenth and fourteenth centuries, whilst the modes were still being used, and consisted entirely of the white notes, C, D, E, F, G, A, B and C. As the augmented 4th, F to B, was felt to be obnoxious, B♭ was introduced by cutting away part of A and B and fitting a short, narrow finger-key in between.

After the B♭ other notes were probably introduced in this order,

---

Music: a Short History, by Evelyn Porter.

F♯, E♭, C♯ and G♯, the modal system began to break up and our modern key system came to be recognized.

In spite of the enormous change in music since that time, the keyboard has altered very little since 1450, except for a little variety in the width of the finger-keys and the colouring of short and long notes respectively as white and black or black and white.

The major advance has been made by the introduction of equal temperament, which enables us to use seven each of naturals, sharps, flats, double sharps and double flats, i.e. thirty-five notes in all, which can all be played on the twelve semitones of the modern keyboard octave.

THE HARPSICHORD FAMILY (*the strings are plucked*)

The earliest form was the psaltery, a stringed instrument which was plucked by a plectrum or with the fingers. This instrument was much in use in the fourteenth and fifteenth centuries.

The VIRGINALS, SPINET and HARPSICHORD proper all have strings lying horizontally. When the finger-keys are depressed, small pieces of wood, called 'jacks', with plectra, rise. These plectra are made of quills or points of leather. They pass the strings, plucking them in passing. The jacks fall back and the plectra, by means of a replacement, do not pluck the strings when they repass them. The tone thus produced is a kind of twang. Unlike the clavichord and the piano, the touch makes very little difference to the tone.

The virginals, or pair of virginals, were very popular in the sixteenth and seventeenth centuries. They have only one string to a note and look like an oblong box. Some can be placed on a table and some have legs. The strings run from right to left and parallel with the keyboard. English Virginal music is very important, the best known being the *Fitzwilliam Virginal Book*.

The spinet has also only one string to a note, but is wing-shaped, the outline following the various lengths of the strings, like the modern grand piano. The strings run from the keyboard at an angle of 45 degrees. The earliest known spinet was made in Philadelphia in 1742. Spinets were popular until the end of the eighteenth century. An upright version was called the CLAVICYTHERIUM.

Another plucked instrument which was swung when played was the BELL HARP, which was invented in the eighteenth century.

The HARPSICHORD itself has two or more strings to a note. It is shaped like a spinet, but the strings run from the keyboard at right angles. The oldest known, dated 1521, is in the South Kensington Museum, London, and has a compass of nearly four octaves.

The number of strings to a note can be varied by mechanical means, such as stops (as in an organ) or pedals (as in a piano), which throw the extra strings in or out of action and otherwise modify the quality of tone. An additional set of strings, tuned an octave above or sometimes an octave below, can then be put into use.

Often there are two keyboards, and occasionally three. Finger touch makes little difference to the tone, although holding the notes down and checking the dampers can sustain the tone.

Many people made and tuned their own instruments. Bach is reported to have tuned his harpsichord in a quarter of an hour. Owing principally to its long, thin strings, the harpsichord required frequent tuning (once weekly) and re-quilling.

The general use of the harpsichord died out with the coming of the pianoforte at the beginning of the nineteenth century.

The modern harpsichord has more mechanical advantages and tonal qualities than that of former times. Wanda Landowska (died 1959) was a great exponent of the twentieth-century revival in harpsichord-playing.

INSTRUMENTS IN WHICH THE STRINGS ARE HAMMERED

The DULCIMER is an ancient instrument. It is a shallow, closed box upon which wires are strung to be struck by small, wooden hammers. The dulcimer was in use in England until the seventeenth century. It is still used by bands in Eastern Europe and the Hungarian name is CYMBALON. Kodaly has used it in *Hary Janos*. The glass dulcimer is a kind of HARMONICA. The PANTALEON was an elaborated dulcimer.

The dulcimer was a forerunner of the CLAVICHORD, which was popular from about the fourteenth to the beginning of the nineteenth century. The earliest had a compass of two and a half octaves.

The clavichord looks like a sort of rectangular box that can be placed upon a table for playing, though sometimes it has legs. One long side of the rectangle has a keyboard and strings run parallel with that side.

Tone is produced by the strings receiving a pressure stroke from below by similarly upward pressed small pieces of metal called tangents. These tangents, or vibrating agents, act as stops when they hit the string, dividing it into two parts. One part is damped and the other is the length which vibrates and produces the required note.

Up to about 1720, tangents, operating adjacent keys, hit the same string, stopping it in different places, so these notes could not be played together. Clavichords operated in this way are called 'fretted'. When playing in commoner keys, this caused no embarrassment, and Bach's *Well-tempered Clavier* has few instances calling for other requirements, although Bach no doubt possessed the newer type of 'unfretted' clavichord with one string to each note.

The tone of a clavichord is soft and ethereal, and mainly suitable for use in a small room as a solo instrument. Unlike the harpsichord, the tone can be modified by touch, and the main tune of a fugue can be brought out, even if it is an inner part. Notes can also be prolonged by a rocking vibration motion of the finger.

The PIANOFORTE is actually a keyed dulcimer, and combines the expressive powers of the clavichord and the loud tone of the harpsichord.

As early as 1430 a French manuscript describes a keyboard instrument with hammers, and a Dutch piano, without dampers, is dated 1610, but the first authentic piano was invented by Cristofori in Florence in about 1709. When a key was depressed it employed an 'escapement' so that after striking a string the hammer returned and left the string free to vibrate. A 'damper' fell on the string and caused it to stop vibrating immediately the finger left the key.

This piano was developed by a German, Silbermann, and played upon by Johann Sebastian Bach. It looked somewhat like the modern grand piano.

Wars in Germany in the eighteenth century drove workmen to England, and Zumpe, a pupil of Silbermann, made an oblong piano which was used by Johann Christian Bach, a son of J. S. Bach. In those times piano frames were wooden and so light that Zumpe's porter could carry one on his back when delivering it.

The upright piano became popular at the beginning of the nineteenth century, but the grand piano, in the shape we know it today, is still considered vastly superior in tone.

Sebastian Erard, a Frenchman, introduced a double escapement action in about 1809, which formed the basis of the action of pianos of today. Pleyel, another Frenchman and a pupil of Haydn, also founded a firm of piano-manufacturers.

An Englishman residing in Philadelphia, John Hawkins, was a pioneer in the use of iron frames in pianos in 1800, but Steinways of Boston made the greatest advances in 1856 with the construction of their first grand with an iron frame as used today. The fuller tone of a piano is obtained by the use of thicker strings, which have to be brought up to a very high tension in order to reach the proper pitch, and pianos require great strength of build to withstand the pull of such strings. A wooden frame would fall to pieces under the drag. Even with iron frames, the stress is mitigated by overstringing—one large group of wires crosses another diagonally—and the piano can be made a reasonable size. This principle was adopted in 1835.

Cristofori's piano had two strings to each note. The average grand piano of today has one string for a few low notes, two strings for about an octave above that and three strings for the remainder of the notes. The very highest notes of about two-inch sounding length have so little resonance that no dampers are used. The lowest strings are wrapped with a copper coiling to increase their mass, and the pitch of the note is determined more by tension than by length. The soft tone of the modern piano is obtained by wool-felted hammers on highly tensed strings.

A large contribution to the tone of a piano is given by the sounding board, which lies under the strings in grands or behind them in uprights. The shape of this becomes altered over years by the pressure of the strings. This explains why the tone of a piano deteriorates with age. The strings and sounding board are connected by a long wooden bridge.

Pianos have two and sometimes three pedals. The right, or sustaining, pedal is the one which removes all the dampers. The notes not only go on sounding, but the ensuing harmonies enrich the tone, although it is normally important to release this pedal and depress it afresh at changes of harmony in order to avoid a confusion of sound.

Lower notes give a greater response to the pedal than upper notes —firstly, because of their larger strings and, secondly, because they awaken harmonies in the notes above them. Half-pedalling is an effect which is obtained by lifting and depressing the pedal very quickly while the lower strings are still sounding. A similar effect is produced by a middle, tone-sustaining, pedal which is attached to most American pianos (perfected by Steinways in 1874). By means of this pedal a note or chord can be held whilst other unheld notes are played at the same time.

The soft pedal acts in several ways. In grands it moves the keyboard and hammers sideways so as to leave unstruck one string of each note. In uprights it moves the hammers nearer to the strings, so that the blow given by them is less powerful. In former times a piece of felt was put between the hammer and the strings.

Cristofori's pianos had a compass of four or four and a half octaves. Mozart's concert grand piano has five octaves. In 1794 Broadwood made the first piano with six octaves. The present usual compass is seven and a quarter octaves.

Touch can either mean the weight of the keys or the manner in which a performer operates them. The weight of a grand is usually from 4½ oz. in the lower keys to 3 oz. in the treble.

The earliest known compositions are by an Italian, Luigi Giustini, who published twelve sonatas for the 'soft and loud harpsichord commonly called the one with hammers' in 1732. Bach and Handel played pianofortes, but wrote for harpsichord and clavichord. Mozart, Haydn and Bach's sons wrote for the piano, but it was Beethoven who really wrote music which brought out the deeper qualities of the instrument. Schumann and Chopin, both born in 1810, wrote vast quantities of music for the piano, obviously finding in it the capacity for conveying romantic thought. Liszt, Brahms, Debussy, Ravel, Poulenc, de Falla, Ireland, Rachmaninoff, Bartók, Stravinsky—these are only a few of the grand number of contributors to the repertory and technique of the piano.

Of course, this repertory includes many early keyboard works actually written for clavichord or harpsichord. It also includes arrangements of orchestral works and compositions for other instruments, for two hands or four, on one or two pianos.

For a practical examination of historical instruments, visit Fenton House, Hampstead, London.

ACTION OF THE MODERN GRAND PIANO

A key A-B consists of a long piece of wood resting on a wooden pivot E at its centre. Only about a third of this piece of wood is covered with a finger-plate of ivory F which can be seen as part of the keyboard.

When the finger depresses a key it causes the long piece of wood to pivot upwards at the other end C and move not only the hammer C-D towards the string BB, but a number of levers with it, which compose its escapement action.

To prevent the hammer from blocking against the string, a set-off nut Q is adjusted so that the horizontal end G of a jack, hopper or L-shaped lever PIOH is tilted against Q at the right moment. As this happens whilst the hammer is still rising, the other end or the vertical part of the hopper slides from under a leather-covered roller, K which is under the end of the hammer furthest away from where it strikes the string. Under this hammer is another lever, the repetition lever, L-M which has been prevented from rising by a screw T at the end of the hammer lever. Therefore, whilst the key is still depressed, the hammer falls back and rests on this lever and a check V close to its felt-covered end U, thus enabling the note to be struck again—facilitating the quick repetition of notes.

When the key is released the hopper springs back to its original position under the roller.

R and S are immovable planks reaching across the full width of the keyboard.

W is the Damper lying on the string.

Y-Z is a crank.

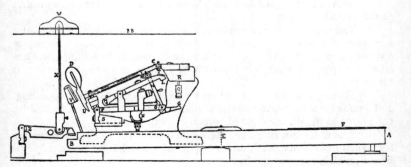

THE ORGAN

The first organ was built by a Greek named Ktesibios or Ctesibios, who lived in Alexandria in the third century B.C. This instrument consisted of an enclosed tank partially filled with water and divided into three interconnecting chambers. The water was pumped into the central chamber, thus increasing air pressure through a wind chute into tuned pipes above. A keyboard was used. An enlarged version of this organ was played by the Romans at their feasts. Such organs were called 'hydraulis'.

After the fall of the Roman Empire, keys disappeared and were only rediscovered in the fifteenth century. From the ninth century onwards large pneumatic organs were used, which were worked by men driving air into the pipes by means of bellows and heavy sliders, with two men working twenty sliders each. A key had to be struck with the fist to produce a note. Hence the name 'organ-beater' for 'organist'.

Owing to the banning of instruments by the Church of Rome, organs were more frequently played in the churches of countries outside Italy. The organ played the notes of the chant and the organum or discanti were added above. These instruments were called 'positive organs'.

Smaller organs were called 'portative organs' and could be moved about. A still smaller kind of reed organ was called a 'regal'. (This is the same family as the mouth-organ, accordion, concertina, harmonium and American organ.)

In Britain, with the Restoration in 1660, many organs were built to replace those destroyed by the Puritans.

The greatest development came in Germany, and pedals appeared there as early as 1448. In France the first pedalled organ was built in the early seventeenth century, but many organs were completely without pedals in England until the late nineteenth century. In 1844 Mendelssohn was prevented from giving a recital because the organ in Hanover Square Rooms did not have German pedals.

However, the swell device was invented in England in 1712.

Many older organs have now been restored in order to play music of the period correctly.

The modern organ consists of a wind-chest, over which are placed a number of pipes. The pipes are in rows, each row a rank; consisting of a set of pipes which give some special tone character. The wind-chest has an even supply of wind driven into it by feeders or an electric-powered rotary fan.

Sliders of wood are placed under the pipes to *stop* them sounding, and knobs or stops placed near the manuals can be operated at will by the player to obtain the desired sound, or register.

The notes can be played from one or as many as seven keyboards for hands called 'manuals', and a keyboard for the feet, called a 'pedal board', which supplies the bass.

The pipes are called, according to length, 2-ft., 4-ft., 8-ft., 16-ft. and 32-ft. stops.

The most important manual is called the 'great organ'. Others are called the 'swell organ', 'choir organ', 'solo organ', 'echo organ', etc.

Two manuals can be played together by using couplers.

The basic tone of the organ is called the 'diapason'. Others have names such as 'flute', 'gamba', 'vox angelica', 'vox humana', etc. The tremulant makes the sound vibrate.

The detached console is the keyboard which is placed away from the pipes, so that the player can hear himself or be in touch with other performers, such as a choir.

CHAPTER ELEVEN

The Orchestra

MONTEVERDI (1567-1643) is probably the father of the modern orchestra, as it was for his operas that instruments of very different character were first brought together: strings (viols of different sizes), woodwind (flutes and oboes), cornetts (the old wooden instruments), trumpets and trombones, a harp, harpsichords, organs and regal (small portable organ)—forty instruments in all.

Soon after this came Purcell (1658-95), when the stringed instruments as we know them were making their way and ousting the viols. In fact, Purcell was criticized for using the 'coarse and loud-toned' violin in preference to the viols. Before Purcell's short life was ended, Bach, Handel and Domenico Scarlatti had all been born in the same year (1685), and now the modern strings became firmly established. For normal orchestral work, trombones had dropped out, but Bach made use of flutes, oboes, oboes d'amore, trumpets and drums, as well as keyboard instruments. The figured bass (continuo) is present, as are all the strings. The other instruments mentioned were never heard all together, but varied from movement to movement. No standard orchestra had yet arrived.

The next change took place about the latter part of the eighteenth and early nineteenth centuries, and here we see the beginnings of a standard orchestra emerging. Haydn (b. 1732), Mozart (b. 1756) and Beethoven (b. 1770) were all composing, and although the numbers of wind employed still varied according to the resources of the court, we find the orchestra settling into two flutes, two oboes, two bassoons, two horns, two trumpets, timpani and strings. The continuo was dropped.

Haydn and Mozart had occasionally used clarinets in symphonic works, and Mozart wrote a concerto for this instrument as well as using it in his operas. He also, for special effects, used trombones in *Don Giovanni* and *The Magic Flute*. Beethoven added two more horns and also brought trombones back into symphonic writing, so that we find Schubert and Brahms composing for a well-established orchestra of two each of flutes, oboes, clarinets and bassoons, four horns, two trumpets, three trombones, timpani and strings.

The next development came in the latter part of the nineteenth century and on into the twentieth. The main layout of the orchestra remained undisturbed, but it became enlarged. Wagner, Strauss, Tchaikovsky, etc., required many more instruments. The piccolo and tuba became an integral part, also the harp and percussion, whilst the strings were increased in number. To the woodwind were added the cor anglais, bass clarinet and double bassoon. French horns at times had eight parts and trumpets three.

This inflation of the orchestra to such gargantuan proportions at the turn of the century (particularly in Europe) and what has happened since are bound up with the life and economics of the times. When the central European states, which had had orchestras and theatres subsidized by the courts of the period of Mozart and Haydn, became Germany, Italy and the Austro-Hungarian Empire, etc., the State supported the existing cultural activities. It can be seen how the impoverishment caused by two world wars has exercised an influence on the orchestra and, because of the added opportunity for performance of works of more modest dimensions, a number of experiments have been made, and a great number of works, including operas, have been written for quite small combinations of instruments.

It is interesting to note that alterations to instruments were at first always made to improve their quality or purity of intonation, or to give them a more complete range of notes, etc. In this generation such is no longer the case. For instance, in the brass instruments the introduction of the German horn has only one asset—that it is easier to play. But as it has a broader bore than the old French horn, it has not quite the same fine quality. The same can be said about the trumpets and trombones, and even the introduction of metal strings, which whilst they may be more practical, are not an improvement in any other way.

WOODWIND INSTRUMENTS

Introduction. The four families that make up the woodwind group which are today in general use in the orchestra are much more varied in tone colour than either the strings or brass sections. We have the *flute* with its almost breathy lower register, rising to a beautifully smooth, lyrical sound and then to great brilliance in its top register. This brilliance of quality is increased in the *piccolo*. The *oboe* is a complete contrast, with much more evenness of quality throughout its smaller range, and the tone is sharper and more biting. In the *clarinet* we have again an instrument of long range, with alterations of quality as it ascends from its lowest register, which is dark and glowing, to its lyrical and brilliant upper tones. The *bassoon* is famed for its dry sound, particularly in staccato notes, although, played legato, it is very telling and, if used with imagination by a composer, can be most effective. All these modern instruments have great facility and can technically respond to the player's wishes in very subtle ways.

Legato playing is obtained by an uninterrupted flow of breath, and staccato by what is called 'tongueing'. This can be single, double or treble tongueing, according to the speed required. The *flutes* have an extra trick called 'flutter tongueing', which is played by rolling the tongue as for a long-drawn-out 'r'.

FLUTE

Forerunners: the fipple flute, recorders and flageolets.

The flute is usually made up of three pieces or joints, although some are made in two pieces only. These pieces are known as the head, body and tail joint, and are normally made of cocus-wood or silver. (Other metals have been used, and ebonite is rare.) The head, plugged at the end, contains the embouchure, or hole for blowing into. The body (and tail joint) contains most of the mechanism for producing the different notes. The fundamental scale of the instrument is D. Two lower notes, C♯ and C♮, are on the instrument, and sometimes the low B. The second octave is obtained by overblowing (an increase in wind pressure) and a third octave in a similar way, with the help of opening certain of the vent

holes. This gives a complete chromatic range of

It is a reedless instrument, the sound being made by the player blowing across the embouchure. The pitch of the notes is controlled by the length of the air column, and this is altered by the opening and closing of the keys. About 1830 *Theobald Böhm* (1794-1881), an inventor and flute player, made important changes in the bore, mechanism and fingering of the instrument, and it is his method that is generally used today.

Piccolo

The piccolo is a small-sized flute on which fingering, etc., is the same, but the compass is an octave higher. It does not play the low C and C♯, and the extremely high B and C are very difficult and can only be played with a loud, piercing tone. It is best to consider its range

as   in actual sounds, although in the score it is written an

octave lower for convenience sake.

Bass Flute

This is called an alto flute on the Continent, and that name is more usual here now, as a further flute has been made which sounds an octave lower. The fingering and compass is exactly the same as for the flute, but being a longer and wider-bored instrument, the range begins a fourth

lower, sounding ♩ The bass flute is infrequently used, but

has been written for by such composers as Rimsky-Korsakov, Glazounov, Holst, Delius, Holbrook, Ravel and Britten.

OBOE

Forerunners: the shalmeys and pommers.

A small, conically-bored pipe of African blackwood which terminates at the lower end in a bell shape. It is a double-reed instrument, and the reed is made of two very fine, thin pieces of prepared cane bound together into a short length of metal tubing called the 'staple'. They are bound so closely together that only the thinnest piece of paper can be inserted between them. The staple is then attached to the top joint of the wood and the player makes the sound by the vibration of these reeds in his mouth, which causes the air column inside the instrument to vibrate. The fundamental scale of the instrument is chromatic from middle C to the C♯ an octave and one note higher. Two lower semitones, B♮ and

B♭, are obtained by key extensions, the next octave

is obtained by overblowing and the top five or six semitones are harmonics of the fundamental octave. The full range of the instrument is

COR ANGLAIS

This instrument may be thought of as an alto oboe and has almost the same range. It is wider and longer, terminates in a small globular bell and at the mouthpiece end the crook is curved. The pitch of the cor anglais is a 5th lower than the oboe and it is a transposing instrument. This means that, although its music is written in the treble clef within this

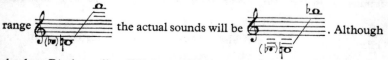

range ⟨ ⟩ the actual sounds will be ⟨ ⟩ . Although

the low B♭ (sounding E♭) is usually omitted, it is added on German instruments.

By writing the music a 5th higher than the sound required the fingering is kept almost the same as for the oboe, and therefore one player can manage both instruments and is often expected to be able to do so as a member of an orchestra. However, the quality of tone differs considerably and the cor anglais is veiled and melancholy in character. There is a beautiful solo for this instrument in *The Swan of Tuonela*, by Sibelius.

CLARINET

Forerunner: chalumeau.

The clarinet is a cylindrical pipe of wood or ebonite two feet long. It consists of five pieces—the mouthpiece, barrel, top joint, lower joint and bell. The underpart of the mouthpiece is flattened to form the 'table', which supports the *single* reed; this is kept in position by a metal ligature. The player, by blowing with pressure of the lips on the tip of the mouthpiece and reed, causes the latter to vibrate, and this in turn causes vibration of the air column through the pipe. The modern instrument has seven holes and an elaborate system of keys, with the aid of which he can obtain a fundamental chromatic scale from E below middle C to B♭ above. Cylindrical instruments overblow at the 12th (and not, as in conical instruments, like the oboe, at the octave). Therefore the notes

from are obtained by overblowing with the aid of a 'speaker' key. A further twelve semitones above this are practical and are harmonics. Clarinets have been built in many keys in the past, but only two, the B♭ and the A clarinet, are constantly in use today. The

chromatic range for both is but they are both

transposing instruments, and the B♭ clarinet sounds a tone lower than

written, thus actually sounding and the A clarinet

sounds a minor 3rd lower than written, thus actually sounding

. (There is also a third and smaller instrument in E♭,

sounding a minor 3rd higher, but it is only rarely used.)

The fingering is the same for both clarinets, but it is usual to use the B♭ one when a piece is in a flat key and the A for sharp keys, as this simplifies the player's task quite considerably. A work in D♭ major written for the B♭ clarinet requires a key signature of only three flats, being written one tone higher in E♭. Similarly, a work in B major would be written for the A clarinet in D major with only two sharps. (If the B♭ instrument was used for this, a key signature of seven sharps or five flats would be needed.) The fingering for the clarinets is very different from the flute and oboe, although the key system in general use is also that invented by Böhm.

Bass Clarinet

This instrument is unique in its quality of sound, and you should listen for it in the 'Sugar Plum Fairy's Dance' in Tchaikovsky's *Nutcracker Suite*. It is really a large-size B♭ clarinet and its written compass

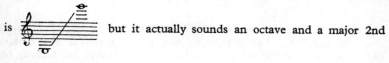

is [notation] but it actually sounds an octave and a major 2nd

lower [notation] . (In Germany it is usually written in the bass clef,

and then sounds only a major 2nd below the written note.) Although the instrument is curved at both ends to accommodate its greater length, the fingering is the same as for the other clarinets.

BASSOON

Forerunner: bass-pommer.

The bassoon is a conically-bored pipe of eight feet doubled back on itself to reduce its length to about four feet. It is made in five pieces —the crook, wing, double joint, long or bass joint and the bell. The crook is inserted into the wing and the double-reed attached to the other end. The reed, though much larger, is very similar to the double-reed of the oboe, which in the modern instrument is almost the only similarity, the quality of tone and characteristics being quite different. The complete

chromatic compass of the instrument is [notation] . The first natural

(or fundamental) octave is [notation] . The second octave to the F

above is obtained by overblowing in the usual manner and the final 7th to the top E♭ by overblowing the fundamental octave at the 12th. The notes from the bottom F to the lowest B♭ are obtained by means of keys. Wagner and Sibelius have written for the low A, and this was obtained by adding another joint to the instrument, but it is not to be recommended.

  In writing for the bassoon, three clefs are used, bass, tenor and treble. The same clefs are used when writing for the 'cello. This is for convenience and to avoid numerous leger lines.

Double Bassoon

  This is the double-bass of the woodwind group. It is seventeen feet in length and in all respects like the bassoon. The modern instrument has a chromatic range 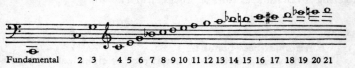 sounding one octave lower than written.

BRASS INSTRUMENTS

  Introduction. The brass instruments of the normal symphonic orchestra today consist of trumpets (sometimes cornets, particularly in France), French horns, trombones and tubas. These instruments have been developed from animals' horns and tusks, through the hunting horns to the modern instruments.

  All are based on a set of notes known as the 'harmonic series'. The intervals of this series blown on a length of tube (which would give C as its fundamental note) are:

Fundamental 2 3 4 5 6 7 8 9 10 11 12 13 14 15 16 17 18 19 20 21

Of these, 7, 11, 13 and 14 would sound out of tune and 17 to 21 be impractical. According to the length of tubing, the fundamental note could be on any degree of the scale, but the player was always restricted to this one series of notes.

  Two major inventions to all the brass instruments (except the trombones) enabled them to take their place in the orchestra, and to keep it.

  First the introduction of crooks. These were pieces of brass tubing of different lengths, enabling the player to alter his fundamental note and series of harmonics, though he was still restricted to only one series at a time.

  Secondly, the invention of pistons and valves, which meant that the instrument became chromatic throughout its entire range. In the days before valves, when crooks were used, theoretically they could be made to allow the player to put his instrument in any key—in fact, crooks for horns were made in B♭ alto, A alto, G, F, E♮, E♭, D, C basso and B♭ basso and the G♭ crook was used once by Haydn in his 'Farewell' Symphony. This led to composers using four horns in two pairs—one pair in the key of the composition and the other pair in, perhaps, the key of the dominant—so providing him with a larger range of notes. It will be seen from this how 'transposing' instruments are part of the normal

procedure of a score. The composer would write

and, according to the key of the composition, would write the direction before it 'Horns in F' or 'Horns in E♭', when it would sound

or . To the player, C-E-G was a

direction to play the 4th, 5th and 6th harmonics. He did the same thing on all occasions and the sound varied according to the crook he used. With the horns, all these crooks transposed downwards from the middle C, the B♭ alto one tone lower and A alto a minor 3rd lower to the C basso one octave lower and B♭ basso, one octave and one tone lower.

In the case of trumpets, those in B♭ and A transposed downwards, but those in D, E♭, E♮ and F upwards, one tone, a minor and major 3rd and perfect 4th respectively.

The introduction of valves did away with all this. The principle is the same, but by the use of valves lengths of tubing are brought into play, lowering the pitch of the fundamental by varying amounts: the first valve one tone, the second valve a semitone and the third valve one and a half tones, which can be used separately or in any combinations and has made the instruments chromatic throughout their range.

TRUMPET

The complete chromatic range of the trumpet today is

. Trumpets are built in A, B♭, C and D. In England B♭

is the most favoured instrument (in some of the older B♭ models a key is added which alters the instrument to A). In France and Italy it is the trumpet built in C which is the most popular. Germany, like England, favours the instrument built in B♭. In America the B♭ and C instruments are used equally. The tone is extremely brilliant and the instrument has great facility.

FRENCH HORN

The modern horn used in the orchestra consists of a spirally-coiled conical tube of brass about twelve feet long. Built in F, with three valves, and played with a funnel-shaped mouthpiece, it was known by the title above. About 1930 the German horn began to be introduced into this country. (It had been in use in Germany since about 1900.) It has become increasingly popular and is now the instrument the student is most likely to see and play. It is of slightly wider bore, and the most popular model is a 'double-rotary' make, which allows the player to be in F or B♭ at will. In other words, two crooks are attached to the instrument. The player would normally use the F crook and bring the B♭ into play for ease and facility on high passages. With the aid of valves to fill in the notes between those of the harmonic series, he has a practical

chromatic range of 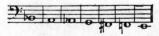 .As it is still usual to write for the

horn in F, these sound a 5th lower. Below this there are certain fundamental notes that can be played.

TROMBONES

Forerunners: the sackbuts.

In the modern orchestra we are concerned with two trombones, the tenor and bass. (Up to the time of Beethoven and Brahms, an alto trombone was also used. It became obsolete, but nowadays some players are using it again.) This instrument is played with a cup mouthpiece and consists of a conical 'bell-joint' with two parallel cylindrical tubes, over which a third U-shaped tube is drawn. This latter is called the 'slide', and it moves up and down the two 'legs'. This alters the length of the column of air vibration. It has seven positions, the first being the shortest, and each lengthened position drops the pitch by one semitone.

The tenor trombone, being built in B♭, has these fundamental notes and accompanying harmonic series:

It is possible to play the 9th and 10th harmonics in the first position, so taking the range up to the second D above middle C. Below the E♮ the first note of the seventh or most extended position of the slide three pedal

notes are possible, those of the first three positions: .

The bass trombone is exactly the same as the tenor, but, as its name implies, it is a lower instrument. In this country it is built in G, on the Continent in F. Therefore its first position is a minor 3rd (in G) or perfect 4th (in F) lower than the tenor. It is usual to write for the bass trombone in the bass clef and the tenor in bass, tenor and alto clefs—occasionally using the treble clef.

The trombone parts are written as they sound and are therefore non-transposing instruments. Experiments have been made with a trombone built in E♭ and B♭ and also with valves, as in the horns, etc., but they are not considered entirely satisfactory and are not in general use in this country, although met with more frequently in Italy.

TUBA

This is a bass brass instrument which has passed through many stages of remodelling in various countries and can only be generally described as the historical descendant of the serpent, the Russian bassoon and the ophicleide group.

Berlioz was perhaps one of the first composers to refer to the tuba, and in his 'Fantastic' Symphony (1830) he used an ophicleide, but in a later edition in 1850 indicated that the tuba could be substituted. However, it was Wagner who developed the position of the tuba in the modern orchestra, although some of his tubas—so-called—were actually modified horns, and from 1869 this mixed family of tubas were established.

The instrument now most commonly in use in English symphony orchestras is the bass tuba in F. It is a true tuba furnished with four valves. The chromatic range is: ⎰⎰⎰ . It is not a transposing instrument and is written for at its proper pitch in the bass clef.

TIMPANI

The modern timpani consist of a bowl-shaped shell of copper (or an alloy) across the top of which is stretched a circular sheet of prepared calf-skin lapped over a wooden hoop and kept in position by a circular iron ring, which can be raised or lowered by T-shaped screws. Thus the tension on the head can be adjusted to allow alterations in pitch. In a modern orchestra it is usual to have four timpani—a large one, two sizes of medium and a small one. The range of any one drum is about a 5th; the exact limits depend on fineness of skin and climate, but we can safely apply these limits:

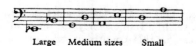

Large   Medium sizes   Small

Composers have written low D and C and the high B♮. A modern development which allows a much faster alteration of notes is what are called 'machine' or 'pedal' timpani. Instead of having to re-tune all the T-screws, the player, by means of a foot pedal, can achieve the same result. It is also possible to obtain a glissando. In Italy a similar improvement has taken place by screwing round the whole bowl.

PERCUSSION

In the modern orchestra this can be a very large group of instruments, some works employing as many as six players. There are twelve instruments in pretty general use, which may be classified in two groups: those with pitch and those without any definite note:

With Pitch
Tubular bells
Glockenspiel
Celesta
Xylophone

Without a Definite Note
Side drum
Tenor drum
Bass drum
Tambourine
Triangle
Cymbals
Gong
Castanets

In addition to these, there are instruments used for special effects, such as the rattle, the wind machine, the anvil, the cuckoo and others borrowed from jazz orchestras: maracas, claves and vibraphone, etc.

Any of these twelve listed instruments can frequently be found and they are described as follows:

WITH PITCH

Tubular Bells. The sets of eight bells are in E♭ major. The intervening semitones can also be added, making the sets thirteen bells in all.

The complete practical range is from

Glockenspiel. This is a series of steel plates, played with two wooden hammers, set in a frame. They are made in different sizes, but the standard pattern in this country is two and a half octaves, G-C (chromatic)— 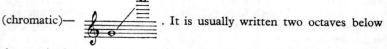 . It is usually written two octaves below

the required sound. There is also an instrument with pianoforte action which is necessary for certain compositions.

Celesta. A keyboard instrument which produces delicate bell-like notes. Small steel plates are set in vibration by hammers controlled from the keyboard, and wooden resonators enhance the beauty of the tone. Its sounding range is from middle C upward for four chromatic octaves, but written one octave lower on two bracketed staves as for the pianoforte. Invented by Mustel of Paris in 1886.

Xylophone. An ancient instrument still in use on the continent in its original form, but English models, used in our modern orchestras are built more efficiently with 27 notes as against the previous somewhat ineffective 36. Bars of rosewood are struck by spoon shaped or round headed beaters. The range, from B♭ (above middle C) upwards chromatically for 27 notes to C in alt, is written with the treble clef.

WITHOUT A DEFINITE NOTE

Side Drum. This is a small instrument, cylindrical in shape, and has a diameter of fourteen and a half inches, but the depth between the two heads varies considerably from three to eight or more inches. The framework is of metal or wood and the heads of prepared calf-skin, like parchment, which are held in position by hoops with brass rods and screws to keep them taut. On the underside are the snares, and these are thin pieces of wire-covered gut stretched across the head, and held by a nut on one side and screw hook on the other. The drum is played with two sticks made of hard wood with a small olive-shaped knob on the end. It can be played with the snares against the head or removed, giving a complete contrast of sound, the one brilliant and the other dull and muffled.

Tenor Drum. The circumference of this drum is almost the same as the side drum, but with much more depth between the two heads, which gives it a deeper and more sombre sound. It is played with sticks similar to the side drum, but has no snares.

Bass Drum. This is a very large drum which gives a deep, booming sound. In the standard concert pattern the wooden shell is cylindrical in shape and has a single parchment head stretched on it. It is played with a large, soft-headed stick and, like the tenor drum, has no snares.

Tambourine. A small wooden hoop over which is stretched a head of parchment. The hoop is cut away at intervals to allow the insertion of small, metal plates in pairs which make a jingling sound. It can be played by shaking it with the hand, by striking the parchment with fingers or knuckles or by rubbing with the thumb around the edge of the parchment.

Triangle. A small length of round steel bent into the shape of a triangle and hit with a rod of the same metal. It makes an extremely clear and pure sound of no definite pitch.

Cymbals. These are two large circular brass plates of equal size. In the centre of each is a saucer-shaped depression to which a strap is attached. The plates are not flat, but tapered, so that when held together they meet only at the edges. They can be played in various ways: by clashing them together (a sideways movement is by far the best); by gently allowing the edges to meet; by suspending one cymbal on a support and hitting with a hard (side drum) stick of with a soft (tympani) stick; or by rolling on the suspended cymbal with a pair of sticks.

Gong. This is a broad, circular plate of hammered metal with the edges turned back all round the circumference. It is usually hit with a hard felt drum stick.

Castanets. These are small hollow pieces of hard wood, usually chestnut (in Spanish, *castaña*) and are a characteristic instrument for accompanying Spanish folk-dances. A pair are usually held one in each hand. For orchestral purposes castanets are mounted at each end of an ebony handle and can then be played without the specialized technique of the dancer. The result is somewhat similar.

HARP

The framework consists of a vertical pillar, curved neck, a comb (which contains the stopping device), a diagonal, semi-conical sounding board and the pedal box. It has a *diatonic* range of over six octaves.

 . It is built in C♭ and has one pedal for each note of the scale—seven in all. These pedals each have two notches cut in the pedal box, and if we take the C♭ as an example (the same thing applies to all the pedals) and depress it to the first notch, it raises *all* the C♭ strings half a tone to C♮, and if we depress it further to the second notch it raises them by one tone to C♯. This is because the stopping device in the comb shortens the vibrating area of the strings by these amounts. The instrument is played by leaning it against the right shoulder and plucking the strings; a glissando can also be played by allowing the thumb or first finger to slide over the strings. It will be seen from the description of the work of the pedals that the same sound can be made on more than one string—C♭ can be made C♯ and the D♭ left. Therefore, if you require a glissando, say, on the dominant chord commencing on B, this can be made up as follows: C♭, D♯, E♭, F♯, G♭, A♮, B♮. Each note therefore, has two strings, except the A♮. Many combinations can be made up in this way.

Harmonics can also be played by stopping the string with the lower part of the hand at a point of equal distance from either end and plucking the string with the finger. This gives a note one octave higher. Arpeggios, chords and glissandi are all equally effective.

Towards the end of the nineteenth century experiments were made with a chromatic harp, and a few composers, including Debussy, wrote for it, but it has not found favour within the orchestra or with harpists.

STRINGS

Introduction. The strings of the orchestra consist of violins, violas, violoncellos and double-basses. (The harp is an instrument with strings, but is not included when you talk of the strings of an orchestra.) All the instruments have four strings and are tuned in 5ths, with the exception of the double-bass, which may have five strings and is tuned in 4ths, except for the fifth string.

It is not necessary to give a detailed description of these instruments, as they are so well known. They all consist of a belly made of soft wood and a back of hard wood, with narrow ribs to prevent the two meeting, but connecting belly and back is the 'sound-post' made of soft wood. Above the body is a neck, ending in a scroll, and the four pegs on which the strings are wound are fitted in position through holes in the neck immediately below the scroll. The finger-board is made of ebony and has a small raised portion called the 'nut' with notches for the strings to rest in, and they are attached to the tail-piece (also made of ebony) at the other end. Between the end of the finger-board and the tail-piece is placed the bridge, which also has notches cut in it for the strings to rest in.

All these instruments are played with a bow, which is drawn across the strings between the end of the finger-board and the bridge, or they can be plucked. The bow is made of very light, pliable wood and strung with horsehair. The hair is attached to the curved wood at one end, and at the 'nut' end (where the right hand holds it) it is caught by a screwed holder, which regulates the tension of the hair. Solidified resin is used to help the bow to grip the strings.

Mutes can be used on all these stringed instruments, and are small, wooden blocks cut to the shape of an M and slit down the legs so that they can be fitted over the bridge in between the strings. The effect is to dampen the vibrations, thereby slightly reducing the quantity of tone and considerably altering the quality.

VIOLIN

The four strings of the violin are tuned as follows:

and the practical range of natural chromatic notes is

A few notes above this are possible, and used, particularly in solo work.

There are two forms of harmonics:

1. Five natural harmonics, obtained by placing the finger lightly on the string at various points, are possible on every string. If you place your finger halfway between nut and bridge you will make a note one octave above the pitch of the open string (the same note is obtained by stopping the string in the same place). By placing your finger on the string at distances one-third and two-thirds from the nut and at one-quarter and three-quarters distance, you will obtain the second and third harmonics. The fourth can be obtained at distances of one-fifth, two-fifths, three-fifths and four-fifths from the nut, and the fifth at one-fifth and five-sixths. It is easy to see that this applies to the other three strings.

Open string   Harmonics

2. Artificial harmonics. These are made by placing the first finger on the note required and stopping it, and then just touching the string a fourth higher with the fourth finger, when the stopped note will sound two octaves higher. This can be done with any stopped note, so that from

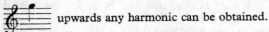 upwards any harmonic can be obtained.

Being the smallest of the stringed instruments, the violin has great facility and can be extremely brilliant. It is about fourteen inches in length and the bow about twenty-nine inches, but both vary a little in size.

VIOLA

The tuning of the viola is one 5th below the violin and its music is written in the alto clef: [image: music notation]. It is, of course, possible to play far higher than the A shown as the top string. Therefore, it also uses the treble clef. The range goes easily from 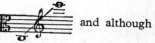 and although

some higher notes can be written for it, it is not to be recommended except for special effect. It is a larger instrument than the violin, but the bow is a little shorter. However, there is more variation in the sizes of violas than of any other of the string group. All the remarks on harmonics, bowing, etc., mentioned under violin apply to this instrument, but we should always remember that it is a larger instrument and, as it is played under the chin, it is a little more awkward to manipulate, particularly in the larger sizes.

VIOLONCELLO OR 'CELLO

The four strings of the 'cello are tuned one octave below the viola: . Like the bassoon, the bass, tenor and treble clefs are

used in writing for the 'cello. The 'cello, of course, is held between the knees and is a very much bigger instrument than violin or viola. But, its construction being on the same lines, all the points of technique mentioned, the different kinds of bowing and harmonics, etc., are the same. Because of its difference in size, for playing above the fifth position the thumb is frequently brought into use. Although the instrument is so much larger than violin or viola, the bow is shorter.

THE DOUBLE-BASS

This is the largest instrument of the string group, but, like the violas, has much more variation in size and shape than the violins or 'cellos. For many years it was a three-stringed instrument, but soon after 1800 the fourth string began making its appearance and the four-stringed instrument is now the most frequently-seen, the three-string instrument having become quite obsolete.

In fairly recent times a five-string bass has been made, and several of these are to be found now, as it is a great advantage to have one or two in an orchestra.

The three-string bass was generally tuned: and when

the fourth string appeared it kept this tuning and added E a 4th below the A. The fifth string, when present, is tuned to the C, a major 3rd below the E, and gives the instrument the same lowest note as the 'cello, but we must remember the sound is one octave lower than written. The bow is now like a 'cello bow, but shorter and stronger. It used to be like

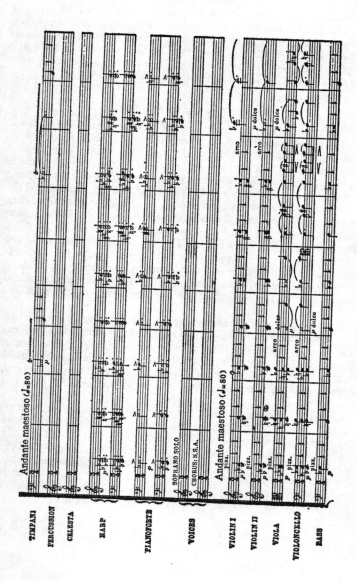

the one used to play 'viols', and was shaped like an archer's bow. Also the position of the hand holding it was reversed, and instead of being on top of the bow was underneath, with the palm turned upwards. Some bass-players abroad still hold it in this way. Natural harmonics are quite easy to play, except on the lowest string (E), but artificial harmonics are only possible on the top string and not often used.

THE ORCHESTRAL SCORE

The layout of the orchestral score has become almost standardized. When Monteverdi gathered his orchestra together, only a figured bass, the voice part and a few indications existed. After that, if we look at scores by Handel we will see that trumpets and drums, if used, come at the top, then perhaps oboes. After that violins, violas, then any voices and 'cellos and basses at the bottom of the page. But in many numbers where just strings and oboes are used, the violins and violas are put first, then the oboes, going on to the voices and basses. In modern printed scores the woodwind are always at the top, starting from the treble to the bass, i.e. flutes, oboes, clarinets, bassoons. The only variation here is in the flutes. If there is a complete piccolo part, that may be the first line followed by the flutes, but if the part is written for the flute and piccolo to be played by one person, then it will be played by the second or third flute-player and be placed underneath the line given to the principal flute.

The next group of instruments is the brass. These do not go from treble to bass, but are in the following order: horns, trumpets, trombones and tuba. The reason for this is because the horns, although brass instruments, do a lot of playing with the woodwind group, and it is convenient to have them next to it. Wagner used to put his bassoons after the horns, presumably considering his horns with the woodwind and the bassoons the basses of the group.

After the brass we come to timpani and percussion, followed by harp, piano, celesta or any other extra instrument used. (If the work includes a voice or voices, that would be next.)

Finally, at the bottom of the page come the strings—like the woodwind, from treble to bass, first violins, second violins, violas, 'cellos and double-basses. The example on pages 130-1 shows this very large layout of a modern score, the *Sinfonia Antartica*, by Vaughan Williams. (Although printed on two pages, the score is read vertically).

CHAPTER TWELVE

Italian Terms

A capella. Unaccompanied choral singing in the church style.

Accelerando. Becoming gradually quicker.

Adagio. Slow, but not so slow as *largo.*

Adagissimo. Slower than *adagio.*

Ad libitum. At will.

Affabile. Affable; in a gentle, pleasing manner.

Affettuoso. Affectionately.

Affrettare. To hurry.

Aggradevole. Agreeable.

Agitato. Agitatedly.

Allargando. Becoming slower and slower.

Allegretto. Quick and lively, but not so fast as *allegro.*

Allegro. Merry; quick; lively; bright.

Al segno. Go back to the sign.

Amabile. Lovable.

Amoroso. Lovingly.

Ancora. Still; again.

Andante. Slowish, but not slow.

Andantino. Usually not as slow as *andante.*

Anima. Soul. *Con anima:* with soul or soulfully.

Animando. Animating.

Animato. Animated.

Animo. Spirit.

Animoso. Spirited.

Appassionato. Impassioned.

Arco. Use the bow.

Ardito. Bold.

Assai. Very; extremely.

Attacca. Attack; start the next movement at once.

Brio. Vigour; spirit; fire. *Con brio:* with spirit.

Calando. Softer and slower.

Calmato. Calmed.

Calore. Heat; passion.

Cantabile. Singing style; smoothly performed and well-brought-out melody.

Cantando. Singing—as *cantabile.*

Canto. Song. *Col canto:* the accompanist to follow the singer.

Canto fermo. The melodic line or plainsong.

Capriccioso. Capricious.

Col. With the. *Colla voce:* with the voice.

Col legno. With the wood.

Commodo. Convenient.

Con. With. *Con sordino:* with mute. (See *brio* for *con brio.*)

Corda. String. *Una corda:* one string or soft pedal. *Tre corde:* three strings or lift soft pedal.

Crescendo. Increasing; becoming gradually louder.

Da. Of; from.

Da capo. Go back to the beginning and start again. *Fine* marks the place at which to finish.

Dal segno. Return to the sign.

Danza. Dance.

Deciso. Decided.

Decrescendo. Becoming gradually softer.

Delicato. Delicate.

Destra. Right. *Mano destra:* right hand.

Diminuendo. Diminishing; becoming gradually softer.

Dolce. Sweet and soft.

Dolcissimo. Very sweet.

Dolente. Doleful; sorrowful.

Dolore. Dolour; pain.

Doloroso. Dolorous; painful.

Espressione. Expression.

Espressivo. Expressively.

Fermata. A pause.

Fine. End.

Forte. Loud.

Fortissimo. Very loud.

Fuoco. Fire; a combination of force and speed.

Furioso. Furiously.

Giocoso. Jocose.

Giojoso. Joyfully.

Giusto. Exact. *Tempo giusto:* strict or suitable time.

Gradevole. Pleasing.

Grandioso. With grandiloquence.

Gravamente. Gravely.

Grave. Slow speed and solemnity.

Grazioso. Graceful.

Insieme. Together; ensemble.

Istesso. The same. *L'istesso tempo:* the same *tempo.*

Lagnevole. Doleful.

Lamentoso. In lamenting style.

Largamente. Broadly; slowish and dignified.

Larghetto. Slow and dignified, but not so much as *largo.*

Largo. Broad; dignified in style.

Legato. Literally meaning bound; passages marked *Legato* should be performed with a smooth connection between the notes.

Leggiero. Light.

Lento. Slow.

Lesto. Quick.

L'istesso tempo. Same speed.

Loco. Place. *Al loco:* At the place.

Lontano. Distant or remote.

Lunga. Long.

Lusingando. Coaxing.

Maestoso. Majestically.

Maggiore. Major.

Marcato. Marked.

Martellando. Hammering.

Marziale. Martial.

Meno. Less.

Mezzo. Half.

Moderato. Moderate in point of speed.

Molto. Much; very.

Molto allegro. Very quickly.

Morendo. Dying.

Mosso. Moved. *Più mosso:* more moved or quicker.

Moto. Motion. *Con moto:* with motion.

Moto perpetuo. A piece which can repeat itself indefinitely.

Niente. Nothing.

Non troppo. Don't overdo it. See *tanto.*

Passionato. Passionate.

Perdendo. Losing; gradually dying away.

Pesante. Weighing; heavy.

Piacere. Pleasure. *A piacere:* at pleasure.

Piacevole. Agreeable.

Piangevole. Sad.

Pianissimo. Very soft.

Piano. Soft.

Più. More.

Più mosso. Quicker.

Pizzicato. Strings plucked with the fingers instead of bowed.

Poco. A little.

Poco a poco. Little by little.

Prestissimo. Very quick.

Presto. Quick.

Primo. First. *Tempo primo: tempo* as at first.

Rallentando. Slowing.

Religioso. Religious.

Rinforzando. Reinforcing individual notes or chords with stress.

Risoluto. Resolute.

Ritardando. Holding back gradually.

Ritenuto. Held back; slower immediately and not gradually, as with *ritardando.*

Ritmico. Rhythmic.

Rubato or *tempo rubato*. The term applies to those tiny little hurryings and slowings in the course of a phrase during performance. In Romantic music of the nineteenth century this became much more marked than heretofore, and is supposed to have helped to convey the romantic feelings of the time.

Scherzando. Jokingly.

Secco. Dry.

Segno. The sign.

Senza. Without.

Senza sordino. Without mute.

Sforzando; sforzato. Forcing; forced; strongly accenting a note or chord.

Sinistra. Left. *Mano sinistra*. Left hand.

Slargando. Slowing up, i.e. the same as *rallentando*.

Smorzando. Making the performance softer and slower to extinction.

Solenne. Solemn.

Sonevole. Sonorous; resonant.

Sopra. On, above.

Sordino. Mute.

Sostenuto. Sustained.

Sotto voce. Literally, under the voice; in an undertone.

Spiccato. *Staccato* effect; a loose, bouncing movement of the bow of a stringed instrument.

Spirito. Spirit; vigour.

Staccato. Detached. (See Chapter 8.)

Stretto. Drawn together, i.e. *accelerando* (*q.v.*). For *stretto* in fugue, see Chapter 14.

Stringendo. Squeezed; the time progressively quickened.

Subito. Suddenly.

Tanto. So much; as much; too much. *Non tanto*: don't overdo it.

Tantino. A very little.

Tedesca. German. *Alla danza Tedesca*: like a German dance.

Tempo. Speed. (See *giusto, primo* and *rubato*.)

Teneramente. Tenderly.

Tenuto. Held, i.e. a note sustained to the end of its value, and perhaps sometimes a little more.

Timoroso. Fearful.

Tranquillo. Tranquil.

Tre corde. Lift soft pedal.

Tremolo. *Tremolo* is the name for the effect caused by the bow of a stringed instrument, and *vibrato* is the name for the effect caused by vibrating the vocal chords.

Tristo. Sad.

Troppo. Too much. *Allegro ma non troppo*: quick, but not too quick.

Tutta; tutte. All; plural.

Tutti. A passage for the whole orchestra.

Una corda. Soft pedal. (See *corda*.)

Un poco. A little.

Veloce. With velocity.

Vibrato. See *tremolo*.

Vivace. Vivacious.

Volti. Turn.

Volti subito. Turn over at once.

Zu 2. (See Chapter 8).

ADDITIONAL TERMS

Alla breve. Two minim beats in a bar indicated thus:- ¢ or $\frac{2}{2}$.

Doppio movimento. Double speed.

Forza. Force.

Glissando. To play a rapid scale passage by drawing the tip of the thumb or finger along the white keys.

Lacrimoso. Tearfully.

Mesto. Gloomy.

Opera comique. Opera in which the spoken word is used.

Opus. Work. Used for listing compositions.

Ostinato basso. A ground bass.

Pomposo. Pompous.

Strepitoso. Noisy.

CHAPTER THIRTEEN

Short Chronology of Musical Events

including some references to wider cultural and historical trends.

TO SHOW THE IMMENSELY rapid rise of organized music in the known history of man, the following chronological information has given rather more space to the earlier periods, about which knowledge is sparse, but which is so important in helping the student to realize how deeply general historical events have influenced the trends in music and shifted its basis from time to time. In Britain, for example, the final invasion by the Normans (themselves alien races from northern Europe, Denmark and Germany) in 1066 altered the musical life of the ruling classes in this country and substituted the French *trouvères* and *jongleurs* for our own minstrels and bards, making the English speech and music unfashionable. Even further back in history, the Church in Rome had, through St. Augustine in the seventh century, imposed her language and musical form upon the religious services in Roman Catholic churches then established—in this country the only Church until after 1534.

Nevertheless, it is certain that in the fields and cottages, and in the servants' kitchens of the masters' castles and manors, the folk-music of the working people continued to be sung and played. Although only passed on orally, it gathered and endured through the ages. After the beginning of the fourteenth century, education, increasing means of transport and scientific invention brought about rapid progress in music and the other arts, hand in hand with the changes of social conditions.

B.C.

3000   Egyptians, Chinese, Chaldeans, Assyrians, Babylonians, Hebrews and Greeks all cultivated music, including singing, choral and solo, and instrumental ensembles accompanying the singing and dancing at religious, military and ceremonial functions.

King David and King Solomon both encouraged the practice of music amongst the Hebrews.

Iberians from Spain and western Europe reached the shores of Great Britain and, at the same time, not later than 1800 B.C. erected the burial ground of Stonehenge.

776   The first Olympic Games, in Greece, at which there were singing and competitions.

676   The seven-stringed *kithara* used to accompany Greek songs.

About this time Britain was invaded by the Celts from northern Europe. Among them were the Gaels, who brought the use of iron,

676 and the Britons. They spread everywhere, imposing their Celtic tongue upon the inhabitants and vigorously practising agriculture, iron smelting and many arts and crafts. Their religion was nature-worship with many gods and superstitions.

540 Pythagoras, Greek philosopher, lectured on musical theory and worked scientifically on the measuring of sound.

Confucius, Chinese sage, collected folk-songs of his native land.

408 Greek philosophers, such as Plato, Aristotle, Aristoxenes, Euclid and Theophrastus wrote about music.

Fragments of the music to the *Orestes* of Euripides, which have been preserved, date from this period.

330 Britain visited by the Greek traveller, Pytheas.

The Celtic tongue was universal.

Contact with Europe constantly maintained for trading purposes, including shipments of tin from the Cornish mines.

200 The Romans took over Greek musical culture and used such instruments as the tuba, cornu, buccina and lituus for military purposes.

54   Julius Caesar made his second attempt at invading Britain.

A.D.

43   The Roman conquest of Britain began. The resulting occupation lasted for nearly 400 years.

63   Religious songs were written by the early Christians and Nero appeared at the Olympic Games in Greece as a singer.

122 Plutarch, Claudius, Ptolemy and others wrote about musical theory.

Hadrian's Wall was being built from Newcastle to Carlisle.

Period of Greek Modes and Plainsong

300 Choral singing developed among the Christians.

380 Ambrose, Bishop of Milan, introduced the so-called Ambrosian chant.

410 Roman garrisons withdrawn from Britain, and invasions by Scots from Ireland, Picts from the north and Saxons from across the North Sea (mainly consisting of the Teutonic races) devastated the country. These races from Europe had pagan religions and began to call themselves the English.

596 Pope Gregory organized the music of the Catholic Church and the Schola Cantorum was founded in Rome.

The Gregorian modes were the basis of the plainchant, which varied in style according to the text and the period in which it was written. It seldom exceeded an octave in compass.

670 Pope Gregory sent St. Augustine to convert Britain to Christianity, which was more or less achieved by about this year.

700 St. John of Damascus organized Russian Church music, the Greek Orthodox Church being the eastern counterpart of the Roman Catholic Church.

Writing became an organized part of religion; thus history and the arts could be recorded.

757 Sacred and secular music cultivated at the Byzantine Court.

793   Danish invasions of Britain and northern France began. These forces
            finally settled mainly in the Midlands, Eastern Counties and
            Yorkshire.
            The Gregorian modes now fully in use and neumes were used to
            indicate pitch.
871   Singing schools founded in Chartres, Cambrai, Nevers, etc.
900   Alfred the Great held Wessex and Mercia.

Period of Medieval Music, including Organum

1026   Part writing in music (organum) developed and the Greek modal
            names were taken over.
            Organs were built in churches and neumes were now used on a stave
            of four lines, devised by Guido d'Arezzo, thus making intervals
            exact instead of vague.
1066   William I of Normandy conquers Britain.
1150   The period of the troubadours, trouvères, jongleurs and ménestrels of
            France, who came over to England during the reigns of William I
            and II and Henry I and II, all of whom came with their conquering
            armies from Normandy.
1180   The musicians of Notre Dame in Paris organized the form of music
            more closely and three- and four-part writing was introduced.
1186   King John of England (youngest son of Henry II) came to the throne
1204   and by 1204 had lost his possessions in Normandy.
            Following his quarrel with the Pope over the appointment of a new
            Archbishop of Canterbury, the Church in England was disrupted
            for seven years.
            After an abortive attempt to regain his lands in Normandy, John
            returned to England, where the disgruntled barons forced him to
1215   sign Magna Carta in June, 1215.
            The German Minnesingers active.
            Chinese composers were writing songs.
1226   The period of the Mystery and Easter plays and the beginning of
            official music instruction at Oxford and Paris Universities.
1240   Date of the well-known canon, 'Sumer is icumen in'.
1270   Adam de la Hale writes his opera, *Jeu de Robin et Marion* in France.

Fourteenth-century Music, including Polyphony

1310   The period of transition from the *ars antiqua* (old music) to the *ars
            nova* (new music), which included a rising interest in secular music.
            England, Wales, Scotland and Ireland now appeared to have separate
            identities and their cultural life began to show some national trends.
1330   Musical forms, such as the rondeau, motet, madrigal, ballata and
            caccia now in frequent use.
1360   Secular and instrumental music for the lute, viol, harp and organetto
            was composed by Guillaume de Machaut in Prague and by Francesco
            Landino in Florence.
1370   The Meistersingers active in Germany.
1373   In England, Geoffrey Chaucer was writing his *Canterbury Tales*,
            establishing an English literature, and travelling to France and Italy.

1373	Also, William Langland, the peasants' poet, wrote *The Vision of Piers Plowman* about this time.
1381	The Peasants' Rising in England.

Fifteenth-century Music, including Modal Harmony

1415	The English musician, John Dunstable, made journeys to Europe and developed a contrapuntal style of great beauty. Many of his manuscripts are preserved in the British Museum.
	Henry V at the Battle of Agincourt.
1416	Guillaume Dufay was a chorister at Cambrai Cathedral and became a leader of the Netherlands school of polyphonic composers.
	Van Eyck [1385–1441], Flemish painter, at the height of his powers.
1428	Italian musicians create secular music and Fra Angelico painted his religious frescoes.
1431	Joan of Arc burnt as a witch at Rouen.
1460	Musical notation improved, and Oxford University conferred the first degree of Doctor of Music on John Hambroys.
1476	Caxton set up his printing press.
1492	Moors driven from Spain.
	Columbus discovered America.
1495	Josquin des Prés was Choirmaster at Cambrai Cathedral, and composed much church music during a long and active life as a practising musician.
1497	Ottaviano Petrucci printed music and music books from movable type in Venice.
	Botticelli and Leonardo da Vinci were painting.
	Two Venetian sailors, John and Sebastian Cabot, sailed from Bristol for Henry VII of England to re-discover North America.

Sixteenth-century Music, including Major and Minor Modes

1500	Josquin des Prés at the Court of Louis XII in Paris.
1501	Petrucci printed a volume of works by Josquin.
1507	Obrecht, Busnois, Agricola active.
	The first lute book published.
1509	Henry VIII encouraged music in England.
1516	Thomas Moore's *Utopia* published.
1520–69	Breughel, Flemish painter.
1524	Johann Walther and Martin Luther published the *Sacred Song Book*.
1527	Pierre Attaingnant printed first chansons in Paris.
1528	Martin Agricola issued his *Musica Instrumentalis*.
1530	Attaingnant printed organ, lute and vocal music.
1542	The first psalms by Clément Marot and L. Bourgeois were issued.
1544	Palestrina (whose name was really Giovanni Preluigi da Palestrina) became Organist and Choirmaster at Palestrina Cathedral at the age of nineteen.
1547–1614	El Greco painted in Spain.

1549	John Marbecke set to music the liturgy of the Book of Common Prayer.
1554	Palestrina wrote his first book of Masses.
	William Byrd was a chorister at St. Paul's, London.
1555	Mary of England persecuted many Protestants in her desire to revive the Catholic faith.
1556	Orlando di Lassus wrote his first book of motets, and in 1560 went to Munich.
	Palestrina composed *Improperia*, and in 1561 was appointed Choirmaster at Santa Maria Maggiore in Roma.
1563	William Byrd became Organist at Lincoln Cathedral.
1564	William Shakespeare born at Stratford. (He died in 1616.)
1567	Palestrina wrote his second book of Masses, including his *Missa Papae Marcelli*.
1570	A study of Greek writers on music was started in Italy.
1571	Palestrina was made Chapel-master of St. Peter's in Rome.
c. 1573	Birth of Ben Jonson. (He died in 1637.)
1575	Thomas Tallis and William Byrd granted a music-publishing monopoly by Queen Elizabeth of England.
1577	Vittoria (*c.* 1540–1611), Spanish composer and friend of Palestrina in Rome, composed motets and Masses.
1580	Nanini and Palestrina founded a music school in Rome.
	Jan Sweelinck was organist at Amsterdam.
1581	Count Bardi of Vernio, Italy, founded the Florentine Camerata and introduced the operatic form.
1583	Jacopo Pari was appointed musical director to Ferdinand I in Italy.
1588	Spanish Armada beaten by the English.
1590	Monteverdi at the Court of Mantua.
1594	Peri's opera, *Dafne*, performed in Florence.
1597	Thomas Morley issues his *A plaine and easie introduction to Practicall Musicke*.

Seventeenth-century Music, including Simple Keys and More Complicated Part Writing

1600	The opera *Euridice*, by Peri and Caccini, performed at Florence at the marriage festivities of Mary de' Medicis and Henry IV of France.
1601	*The Triumphs of Oriana* issued by Thomas Morley, and *Julius Caesar*, by Shakespeare, was published.
1604	Caccini visited Paris.
	Othello, by Shakespeare, published.
1605	The first part of Cervantes's *Don Quixote* published.
1606	Rembrandt born at Leyden in Holland.
1608	The opera *Ariadne* produced in Mantua, with recitatives by Peri, arias by Monteverdi and text by Rinuccini.
	Frescobaldi became Organist at St. Peter's in Rome and composed instrumental works in 1627.
1609	First book of catches, rounds and canons printed in England, entitled *Pammelia* and published by Thomas Ravenscroft.
1610	*The Alchemist*, by Ben Jonson, published.

1611   *Parthenia*, containing music for virginals published by Byrd, Bull and Gibbons, and Shakespeare's *The Tempest* and *The Winter's Tale* published.

1627   *Daphne*, first German opera, by Heinrich Schütz, produced at Dresden.

1632   Rembrandt painted *The Anatomy Lesson of Professor Tulp*.

1642   Monteverdi's last opera, *Coronation of Poppea*, produced in Venice.
     Galileo, mathematician, physicist and astronomer died in Florence a few years after having been forced by the Inquisition to contradict his theory that the earth moves round the sun and not vice versa.
     Puritan influences closed the theatres in London.

1643   Deaths of Monteverdi and Frescobaldi.

1645   Lully violinist and kitchen boy at French Court.
     Italian operas performed in Paris, and Heinrich Schütz composed his *Seven Words of Christ on the Cross*.

1649   Charles I of England beheaded at Whitehall, London.

1653   Lully made Court Composer to Louis XIV and Director of the Paris Opéra.

1655   Cromwell organized the conquest of Jamaica.

1656   *The Siege of Rhodes*, first English opera, performed in London, and composed by Locke, Lawes, Cooke, Coleman and Hudson, with libretto by William Davenant.

1659   The opera, *La Pastorale*, by Robert Cambert (1628–77), produced in France.

1660   John Jenkins published twelve sonatas for two violins and bass, with a thorough-bass for the organ or theorbo.
     Henry and William Lawes composed music for the English masques.

1662   The slave trade in West Africa became a lucrative business.

1663   The blind Milton wrote *Paradise Lost*.

1665   Schütz composed his *St. John Passion*, and England was devastated by the Great Plague.
     Building of the Louvre, Paris, begun.

1666   The Fire of London.

1668   The East India Company acquired Bombay, India.
     Building of Palace of Versailles begun.
     Dryden made Poet Laureate of England.

1669   Molière wrote *Tartuffe*.

1671   First opera-house in Paris opened.
     Johann Ambrosius Bach (J. S. Bach's father) active as organist at Eisenach.

1672   Popular concerts established by John Banister in London.

1675   Christopher Wren began to rebuild St. Paul's Cathedral after its destruction in 1666.

1677   Racine wrote *Phèdre*.

1678   First German opera-house at Hamburg.

1680   Henry Purcell made organist at Westminster Abbey.
     String instruments became popular and music for violins and 'cellos increased.

1685   J. S. Bach, G. F. Handel and Domenico Scarlatti born.
     Dryden's opera, *Albion*, performed.

1686	Lully composed his last opera, *Armide*, and died in Paris in 1687.
1688	Purcell's *Dido and Aeneas* produced in London.
	Johann Kuhnau issued his *Clavier Studies*.
1693	Couperin active as Court organist in Paris.
1698	Alessandro Scarlatti's operas produced in Rome, and Torelli composed the first violin concerto.

Eighteenth-century Music with Additional Harmonic Vocabulary.

1700	J. S. Bach, aged fifteen, studying at Lüneburg.
	Corelli composed twelve sonatas for violin and piano, and violins, violas and 'cellos were being made by Stradivarius and his pupils in Cremona.
1702	Joseph Sauveur, French acoustician, wrote a monograph on musical acoustics.
1703	J. S. Bach violinist in Weimar orchestra, and later called to Armstadt as organist.
	Peter the Great founded St. Petersburg.
1704	Handel composed a Passion and Bach wrote his first cantata.
1705	Handel's first opera, *Almira*, produced in Hamburg, and Bach travelled to Lübeck to hear Buxtehude play the organ.
1706	Rameau published his first book of harpsichord pieces.
1707	Handel's journey to Italy.
1708	Bach active at Weimar as organist and composer.
	Handel composed oratorios for performance in Rome.
1709	Handel and Domenico Scarlatti held organ- and harpsichord-playing contest in Rome.
	Bartolommeo Cristofori built the first pianoforte.
1710	Thomas Arne born, and Handel arrived in England and composed *Rinaldo*.
	St. Paul's Cathedral completed.
1711	Handel returned to Hanover.
	The tuning-fork invented by John Shore.
1712	Jean Jacques Rousseau, Swiss philosopher and musician, born. He lived and worked in France.
1713	Couperin composed four books of harpsichord pieces, and Vivaldi directed the Conservatory della Pietà at Venice.
1714	Rameau organist at Lyons.
	Gluck born at Erasbach.
1715	Domenico Scarlatti made *maestro* at St. Peter's, Rome.
1717	Couperin writes *L'art de toucher le clavecin*.
1719	J. S. Bach visited Halle, but failed to meet Handel there.
	D. Scarlatti visited London.
1720	D. Scarlatti's *Narciso* performed in London.
	Handel composed the oratorio, *Esther*.
1721	J. S. Bach married Anna Magdalena and composed the six *Brandenburg Concertos*.
1722	J. S. Bach composed Book I of The *Well-tempered Clavier*.
1723	J. S. Bach went to Leipzig as Cantor at the Thomasschule and composed the *St. John Passion*.

1724	Handel composed *Tamerlano*, and the Festival of the Three Choirs of Gloucester, Hereford and Worcester was founded.
1726	Jonathan Swift published his *Gulliver's Travels*.
1727	*The Beggar's Opera*, by Gay and Pepusch, produced in London.
1729	J. S. Bach's *St. Matthew Passion* performed in Leipzig on Good Friday.
1732	Gluck studied violin, organ and harpsichord, and Joseph Haydn born at Rohrau.
	William Hogarth issued series of engravings.
1733	Pergolesi composed *La Serva Padrona*.
1735	William Hogarth engraved his *Rake's Progress*.
1736	Vivaldi composed twelve string trios, and Handel composed *Alexander's Feast*.
	Gluck went to Vienna and Milan.
1737	Rameau composed *Castor et Pollux*, and Gluck studied with Sammartini in Rome.
1738	Thomas Arne composed incidental music to Milton's *Comus*.
	J. S. Bach composed his B minor Mass.
	The Royal Society of Musicians founded.
1739	John Wesley began his life's work as an open-air preacher in England.
1740	D. Scarlatti visited London and Dublin, and Joseph Haydn went to Vienna as chorister at St. Stephen's Church.
	Arne composed 'Rule Britannia', which was included in his masque, *Alfred*.
1741	Gluck composed *Artaserse* and Handel finished *Messiah*.
1742	First performance of Handel's *Messiah* in Dublin.
	J. S. Bach's 'Goldberg' Variations printed.
1744	Book II of J. S. Bach's *Well-tempered Clavier* issued.
1745	Gluck went to London.
	The Pretender to the English throne, Prince Charles, reached as far south as Derby with his army of Jacobites and Highlanders.
1749	J. S. Bach composed the *Art of Fugue*.
	Rameau's *Zoroastre* produced in Paris.
	Handel composed *Solomon* and the *Fireworks Music*.
	Henry Fielding published *Tom Jones*.
1750	J. S. Bach died in Leipzig.
1751	Handel became blind.
	Robert Clive, having left the service of the East India Company in India for the British Army, successfully took the province of Arcot in Madras from the French.
1752	Gluck composed *La Clemenza di Tito*, and an Italian opera company called 'Les Bouffons' appeared in Paris.
1753	Rousseau issued his *Lettre sur la musique française*.
1754	George Washington (a descendant of English emigrants of the middle seventeenth century), sent to warn French off settlement in Ohio, North America.
1755	Haydn composed his First String Quartet.
1756	Wolfgang Amadeus Mozart born in Salzburg, and his father, Leopold, issued his *Violin Method*.

1756	Frederick II of Prussia (nephew of George I of England) advanced on Dresden and wrested Saxony from Austria. The Seven Years' War (1756–63) between Frederick and Maria Theresia, Empress of Austria, began.
1757	D. Scarlatti died in Naples.
	Frederick victorious in Prague.
	Clive seized Plassey in Bengal and laid the foundation of British domination in India.
1758	Voltaire wrote *Candide*.
1759	Handel died in London. William Blake born; also Robert Burns.
1760	William Boyce started his collection of old English church music, *Cathedral Music*.
	George III, Elector of Hanover, became King of England.
1762	Gluck's *Orfeo ed Euridice* produced in Rome.
	Mozart's first concert tour, and Thomas Arne's *Artaxerxes* performed in London.
1763	Catherine II became Empress of Russia.
	The Seven Years' War ended in Frederick II's favour.
	England predominant in North America and India, and the French lost hope of a colonial empire.
1764	Rameau died, and Mozart met Johann Christian Bach in London.
1765	Mozart composed his first symphony.
	Baldassare Galuppi appointed Music Director to Catherine III of Russia at St. Petersburg, where he produced his opera, *Ifigenia in Tauride* and others.
	The iron industry established in Merthyr-Tydvil, Glamorganshire.
1766	James Hargreaves, an illiterate weaver, invented the spinning-jenny.
1767	Mozart composed his first opera, *La Finta Semplice*, and Gluck's *Alceste* was produced in Vienna.
1768	Maria Theresia abolished trials for witchcraft.
1769	Mozart visited Italy.
1770	Ludwig van Beethoven born in Bonn, and Handel's *Messiah* was performed in New York.
1771	Piccinni composed *Antigone*.
1772	First German performance of *Messiah* at Hamburg, and Haydn composed his 'Farewell' Symphony.
1774	Gluck's opera, *Iphigénie en Aulide* performed in Paris.
	Death of Louis XV of France. His grandson, Louis XVI, crowned.
1775	Jane Austen born.
	France recognized the United States of America.
	Italy divided into states.
1776	Fierce altercations developed in Paris between the rival factions of Piccinni and Gluck.
	Dr. Charles Burney's *A General History of Music in four volumes* published.
1777	Sheridan's *School for Scandal* performed.
1779	C. P. E. Bach wrote piano sonatas.
1780	Paisiello's opera, *The Barber of Seville*, composed for St. Petersburg.
1781	Mozart's *Idomeneo* produced in Munich.

1781	Johann Hiller presented a new concert series at the Gewandhaus in Leipzig.
	Horatio Nelson, under Lord Hood, patrolled American waters.
1783	Beethoven composed three piano sonatas, and Mozart his Mass in C minor.
	Periodicals now published frequently in Germany on the subject of music.
1784	Italian opera increasingly popular in St. Petersburg, and Beaumarchais wrote his play, *The Marriage of Figaro*.
1785	Haydn composed the *Seven Words of Christ*, and Beethoven wrote his early Piano Quartet.
	Steam engine first used.
1786	Mozart's *Marriage of Figaro* performed in Vienna and Prague.
	Dittersdorf's Singspiel *Doktor und Apotheker*, performed in Vienna.
	Robert Burns wrote some of his poems.
1787	Mozart's *Don Giovanni* performed in Prague, and Gluck died in Vienna.
1788	Mozart composed his last symphonies and his D major Piano Concerto.
	Lord Byron born in London.
1789	Outbreak of French Revolution. On 14th July the Bastille was stormed.
	William Blake wrote *Songs of Innocence*.
1790	Haydn completed his twelve 'London' symphonies for his first visit to that city and also received a doctorate at Oxford.
	Goethe published *Faust*.
	Hereditary titles abolished in France.
1791	John Wesley died after fifty years of Methodist preaching.
	Mozart died in Vienna leaving his *Requiem* unfinished.
	The Berlin Singakademie founded.
1792	Beethoven visits Vienna to study with Haydn and others.
	Rossini born in Pesaro.
	The Marseillaise composed by Rouget de Lisle.
	Percy Bysshe Shelley born.
	England declared war on Austria. Later Prussia joined Britain.
1793	Execution of Louis XVI and, later, of Marie Antoinette. Robespierre First Minister.
	Lord Nelson engaged in storming Corsica in the Mediterranean.
1794	Robespierre arrested and executed.
	Napoleon directed military campaign in Italy.
1795	Beethoven composed his Trios, op. 1, dedicated to Haydn.
	The Paris Conservatoire organized by Bernard Sarretti.
	John Keats born.
	Bread riots in England.
1796	The art song form became popular.
	Paul I became Tsar of Russia in succession to his mother, Catherine II.
1797	Franz Schubert born near Vienna, and Cherubini's *Medea* was performed in Paris.
	Napoleon attacked Egypt in an attempt to strike a blow at England.
1798	Beethoven composed his op. 13, the 'Pathétique' Sonata.
	Russian Army drove French from North Italy.
	Lord Nelson annihilated the French Fleet in the Bay of Aboukir, and was created Duke of Brontë by the King of Naples.

1798   Samuel Coleridge wrote *The Rime of the Ancient Mariner*.
1799   Haydn's *Creation* performed in Vienna.
        Napoleon appointed First Consul in Paris, and Pope Pius VI captured
        by the French and expatriated from Rome.

The general trends during the nineteenth century were towards liberalism and nationalism, demanded by the mass of the people and guided or resisted by the governments in power. The Divine Right of Kings, generally accepted since the sixteenth century, was now discredited, and instead the people themselves gathered confidence and wished to promote their own leaders. The French Revolution established ideas which continued in men's minds after its collapse, and the Industrial Revolution in England brought to the fore-front the injustices of a society divided between a few rich and many poor.

Poets and writers, such as Blake, Shelley, Keats, Byron and William Morris, spoke passionately of these social evils, and some musicians were influenced to comment on them in their compositions—for example, Mozart in his *Marriage of Figaro* and Beethoven in his *Fidelio*.

Possibly owing to their dependence on the patronage of the wealthy, musicians had not been so outspoken as they were to become during the nineteenth and twentieth centuries.

There was great progress in the perfecting of the technique of musical instruments, which added to the vocabulary of expression from which composers could draw inspiration. Chopin and Liszt, for instance, exploited the perfected range of the pianoforte. Orchestral instruments were individually developed, and their variety of colour consciously used for special effects. The nuances of the human voice were exploited by the *Lieder* writers of Germany and the operatic composers of Italy, Russia, France and Germany.

The nineteenth century continued to amass even greater quantities of musical compositions and events, much more than this small volume can cover. The following pages will attempt to note first performances of some of the most outstanding and influential operas, oratorios and symphonies, etc., in conjunction with a sketched-in background of political and social events in which all thinking artists must in some way have become involved.

The twentieth century has brought a new trend in large parts of the world, personified in the U.S.S.R. This is a development of ideas of government support already in existence in several other countries, including our own, but carried a stage further by guaranteeing the individual artist freedom from financial worry in return for his work.

1800   Beethoven composed his First Symphony (op. 21), the first series of
        string quartets (op. 18) and his C minor Piano Concerto.
1801   Lord Nelson attacked the Danish Fleet off Copenhagen.
        Haydn's *The Seasons* performed in Vienna and *The Creation* in Paris.
1802   Peace Treaty signed at Amiens between France and England.
        The St. Petersburg Philharmonic Society founded.
        Beethoven composed his Piano Sonata, op. 31.
        Byron wrote *Childe Harold*.

1803   Beethoven's Second Symphony played in Vienna.

1804   Napoleon crowned Emperor of France and King of Italy by Pope Pius VII.

Beethoven rescinded his dedication of the 'Eroica' Symphony to Napoleon.

1805   Lord Nelson loses his life in victory at Trafalgar over the French and Spanish Fleets.

Beethoven's *Fidelio* performed in Vienna during the first week of French occupation of the city, and withdrawn after three performances.

1806   Beethoven completed his Fourth Symphony, the Violin Concerto, the 'Leonora' Overture no. 3 and the 'Rasumovsky' quartets.

The Holy Roman Empire dissolved.

1807   The Milan Conservatory founded.

Beethoven completed his *Coriolanus* Overture, Mass in C major and 'Appassionata' Sonata.

1808   Beginning of Peninsular War between the French on the one hand and the Spanish, Portuguese and British (chiefly under Wellington) on the other.

First performances of Beethoven's Fifth and Sixth Symphonies in Vienna.

1809   Haydn died in Vienna.

1810   Regency of George, Prince of Wales, in England.

Beethoven wrote music for *Egmont*.

1811   Weber's *Abu Hassan* performed in Munich.

The Prague Conservatory opened.

1812   Napoleon driven out of Moscow.

Mozart's *Don Giovanni* performed in England.

1813   Beethoven's Seventh Symphony performed.

London Philharmonic Concerts begun.

Rossini's *Tancred* performed in Venice.

Jane Austen wrote *Pride and Prejudice*.

1814   Napoleon banished to Elba, and Peninsular War ended in defeat for the French.

Beethoven's Eighth Symphony performed.

John Field's *Nocturnes* for piano issued.

1815   Napoleon finally routed at Waterloo and sent to St. Helena.

The Congress of Vienna.

Maelzel introduced his metronome.

Austria, Russia, France and Prussia formed the Holy Alliance.

1816   Lord Byron left England for the last time.

Rossini's *Barber of Seville* performed in Rome.

Schubert wrote his song 'The Erl King' and Beethoven composed the song-cycle 'An die ferne Geliebte'.

1817   Clementi's *Gradus ad Parnassum* issued in London.

1818   Schubert at the summer home of Count Esterházy, and Chopin played a concerto at a public concert, aged eight.

1819   Schubert composed his 'Forellen' Quintet.

Weber wrote his *Invitation to the Dance*.

1819   Peterloo, the name given to a revolutionary gathering at Manchester, calling for Parliamentary reform, which ended in a merciless attack by the military.

         Employment of children in Britain under nine forbidden in cotton factories.

         Sir Walter Scott wrote *The Bride of Lammermoor*.

1820   Death of George III of England. George IV crowned King of England and of Hanover.

         Beethoven's increasing deafness became almost total.

         Liszt made first appearance as pianist at Ödenburg and studied with Czerny and Salieri.

         Shelley wrote *Prometheus Unbound*.

1821   Weber's *Der Freischütz* performed in Berlin.

         Cherubini became Director of the Paris Conservatoire.

         The Vienna Conservatory opened.

1822   Schubert wrote his 'Unfinished' Symphony.

         Royal Academy of Music opened in London.

1823   Sir Robert Peel established the Metropolitan Police Force.

         Schubert composed his 'Schöne Müllerin' song-cycle.

1824   Liszt visited London and played on the new piano invented by Erard.

         Trade unions allowed to function legally in England.

         Charles X became King of France following the death of his brother, Louis XVIII.

1825   The Thames Tunnel commenced by Sir Mark Brunel and his son, Isambard.

         Chopin's first published work appeared, Rondo in C minor, op. 1.

         Mendelssohn composed his String Octet, op. 20.

1826   Weber's *Oberon* performed in London, and death of the composer.

1827   Beethoven died in Vienna.

         Schubert wrote his 'Winterreise' song-cycle.

         Liszt settled in Paris.

         Wagner studied in Dresden.

1828   Auber's *Masaniello* performed in Paris.

         Schubert died in Vienna.

         Schumann studied at the Leipzig Conservatory.

         Hummel and Czerny issued their piano method.

1829   Rossini's *William Tell* performed in Paris.

         Mendelssohn conducted Bach's *St. Matthew Passion* in Berlin.

         Berlioz composed his *Symphonie Fantastique*.

         Chopin composed his first etudes and was very successful as concert pianist.

1830   The July Revolution in Paris sent Charles X into exile at Holyrood Palace, Edinburgh. His son, Louis Phillipe, the so-called 'citizen' King, elected in his place.

         Chopin gave farewell concerts in Warsaw.

         Auber's *Fra Diavolo* performed in Paris.

         George IV of England died, and William IV, son of George III, succeeded him.

1831   Bellini's *La Sonnambula* performed in Milan.

         Chopin arrived in Paris, and Schumann wrote an article praising him.

1832 Bellini's *Nonna* performed in Milan.
   Keats died in Rome, aged twenty-six.

1833 Slavery abolished in the British colonies.
   Mendelssohn became Musical Director at Düsseldorf, and Donizetti composed *Lucrezia Borgia*.

1834 The Poor Laws in England reformed, and the Tolpuddle Martyrs transported for seven years for trying to organize agricultural workers in Dorset.
   Schumann founded his music periodical, *Neue Zeitschrift für Musik*.
   Chopin played a duet with Liszt.

1835 Donizetti's *Lucia di Lammermoor* performed in Naples.

1836 Meyerbeer's *Les Huguenots* performed in Paris, and Glinka's *Life for the Tsar* in St. Petersburg.
   Mendelssohn's *St. Paul* at Düsseldorf.

1837 Death of William IV of England. Victoria, his niece, succeeded him.
   Alexander Pushkin, Russian poet and dramatist and author of *Boris Godunov, Eugen Onegin* and *Russlan and Ludmilla*, died as result of a duel.

1838 Chopin, very ill with tuberculosis, spent the winter at Majorca.
   Wagner started work on *Rienzi*.
   Schumann discovered Schubert's C major Symphony.

1839 Wagner went to Paris and Liszt toured Europe as concert pianist.
   Chopin's Twenty-four Preludes, op. 28, published.

1840 Wagner wrote his *Faust* Overture and met Liszt in Paris.
   Adolphe Sax invented the saxophone.
   Smetana went to Prague.
   Donizetti's *Daughter of the Regiment* performed in Paris, and Mendelssohn's *Hymn of Praise* at Leipzig.

1841 Schumann wrote his First Symphony.
   Liszt's *Années de pélérinage* published.
   Wagner composed *The Flying Dutchman*.
   Auber's *Crown Diamonds* performed in Paris.
   Delacroix painted *Fall of Constantinople*.

1842 Glinka's *Russlan and Ludmilla* performed in St. Petersburg, and Wagner's *Rienzi* in Dresden.
   Meyerbeer became Musical Director in Berlin.
   Verdi composed *Nabucco*.

1843 Donizetti's *Don Pasquale* performed in Paris, and Balfe's *Bohemian Girl* produced in London.
   Verdi composed *I Lombardi*.
   Mendelssohn founded the Leipzig Conservatoire.

1844 Verdi's *Ernani* performed in Venice.
   Schumann toured Russia.
   Berlioz published his book on instrumentation.

1845 Wagner's *Tannhäuser* performed in Dresden, and William Henry Fry's *Leonora* in Philadelphia.
   Wallace's *Maritana* performed in London.
   Schumann wrote his Piano Concerto, and Liszt wrote the symphonic poem, *Les Préludes*.

1846 Berlioz completed *Damnation of Faust*.

1846	Mendelssohn composed *Elijah*.
	Wagner conducted Beethoven's Ninth Symphony, the 'Choral', in Dresden.
1847	Flotow's *Martha* performed in Vienna.
	Verdi composed *Macbeth*.
	Manuel Garcia wrote his vocal method, *Traité complet du chant*.
	Charlotte Brontë wrote *Jane Eyre*, and Emily Brontë *Wuthering Heights*.
1848	Liszt became Court Music Director at Weimar.
	Smetana opened a music school in Prague.
	Wagner completed *Lohengrin*.
	The February Revolution in Paris and Louis Philippe flees.
	Revolutionary movements in Germany, Poland and Italy.
	Louis Napoleon, nephew of the first Emperor, returned to France and was elected President, assuming headship of the Republic, having won the support of the Army.
	Nicolai's *Merry Wives of Windsor* performed in Berlin.
1849	Chopin died in Paris.
	Wagner forced to leave Dresden.
	Verdi composed *Luisa Miller*.
	Meyerbeer's *Le Prophète* produced in Berlin.
	William Sterndale Bennett founded the London Bach Society.
	Wagner started writing his musical articles, 'Art and Revolution' and 'The Art-work of the Future'.
1850	Schumann went to Düsseldorf as Musical Director.
	The Bach Society was founded in Leipzig.
	Liszt conducted Wagner's *Lohengrin* at Weimar.
1851	Verdi's *Rigoletto* performed in Venice.
	Schumann's Third Symphony performed in Düsseldorf.
	Harriet B. Stowe wrote *Uncle Tom's Cabin*.
1852	Louis Napoleon assumed the title of Emperor.
	Berlioz visited London.
	The 'Music of the Future' school arose under the guidance of Liszt.
1853	Louis Napoleon married the Countess Eugénie of Spain.
	Verdi's *Il Trovatore* performed in Rome, and *La Traviata* in Venice.
	Schumann wrote his article, 'New Paths'.
1854	Turkey, Britain and France declare war on Russia in the Crimea.
	Brahms composed his first songs and the B major Piano Trio.
	Berlioz's *Childhood of Christ* performed in Paris.
1855	Fall of Sevastapol.
	Wagner conducted in London.
	Verdi composed *Sicilian Vespers*.
	Bruckner organist at Linz Cathedral.
	Johann Strauss, Jun., gave summer concerts in St. Petersburg.
	Berlioz conducted Liszt's E♭ major Piano Concerto at Weimar with the composer as pianist.
	Crystal Palace Concerts started in London.
	Anthony Trollope began his Barchester Chronicles.
	Longfellow wrote *Hiawatha*.
1856	Victory of Allies over Russia.

1856   Italy united.
        Liszt finished his 'Dante' Symphony.
        Dargomijsky's *Russalka* performed in St. Petersburg.
        Stuttgart Conservatory founded.

1857   The nine symphonic poems of Liszt published, and Wagner wrote an
            article commenting on them.
        George Eliot began *Adam Bede*.
        Flaubert wrote *Madame Bovary*.

1858   William I (Emperor of Germany) appointed regent to his brother,
            Frederick William IV King of Prussia.
        Cornelius's *Barber of Baghdad* performed in Weimar, and Offenbach's
            Orpheus in the Underworld in Paris.
        Grieg studied at the Leipzig Conservatory.
        Moniusko conducted the Warsaw Opera.

1859   Gounod's *Faust* performed in Paris.
        Verdi's *Masked Ball* in Rome.
        The Russian Music Society formed in St. Petersburg.
        The Handel Festival in London employed 2,700 singers and 460
            instrumentalists.
        Brahms played his First Piano Concerto in Leipzig.
        Liszt left Weimar and went to Rome.
        Wagner completed *Tristan und Isolde* at Lucerne.

1860   Wagner returned to Germany.
        George Eliot completed *The Mill on the Floss*.

1861   Serfs freed in Russia by decree of Alexander II.
        Wagner's *Tannhäuser* produced in Paris.

1862   Benedict's *Lily of Killarney* performed in London.
        Victor Hugo wrote *Les Miserables*.
        Verdi's *Forza del Destino* performed at St. Petersburg.
        Anton Rubinstein founded the St. Petersburg Conservatory.
        Köchel issued his catalogue of Mozart's works.

1863   Fry's *Notre Dame de Paris* performed in Philadelphia, and Berlioz's
            The Trojans, Part II, in Paris.
        Bizet composed his *Pearl Fishers*.
        Tchaikovsky went to the St. Petersburg Conservatory.
        Period of Impressionist painting in France begins.

1864   International Working Men's Association (the First International)
            founded.
        Wagner aided by King Ludwig of Bavaria.
        Tchaikovsky composed his *Romeo and Juliet* overture.
        Max Bruch composed his G minor Violin Concerto.

1865   Von Bülow conducted *Tristan und Isolde* at Munich.
        Liszt became an *abbé*.
        Meyerbeer's *L'Africaine* performed in Paris.
        Lewis Carroll wrote *Alice in Wonderland*.

1866   Smetana's *Bartered Bride* performed in Prague.
        The Moscow Conservatory opened under the direction of Nicholas
            Rubinstein.

1867   Gounod's *Romeo and Juliet* performed in Paris.
        Verdi composed *Don Carlos* and Sullivan *Cox and Box*.

1867	Borodin completed his Symphony in E♭.
	The Copenhagen Conservatory opened.
	Austro-Hungarian Empire formed under Francis Joseph, Emperor of Austria and King of Hungary.
1868	The Trades Union Congress established in Britain.
	Wagner's *Die Meistersinger* performed in Munich, and Boito's *Mephistofele* in Milan.
	Grieg composed his Piano Concerto.
	Smetana composed *Dalibor*.
	Tolstoi finished his *War and Peace*.
	Louisa Alcott wrote *Little Women*.
1869	Social-Democratic Labour Party formed in Germany.
	Wagner's *Das Rheingold* produced in Munich.
	Bruckner composed his Mass in F minor.
	R. Blackmore wrote *Lorna Doone*.
1870	Franco-Prussian War ended in defeat of Louis Napoleon and the occupation of Paris. France became a republic.
	Wagner's *Die Walküre* performed in Munich.
	Gounod goes to London and Grieg visits Liszt in Rome.
	Delibes's ballet *Coppélia* produced in Paris.
1871	Alsace and Lorraine ceded to Germany.
	Verdi's *Aïda* performed in Cairo.
	Rimsky-Korsakov taught composition at the St. Petersburg Conservatory.
	Wagner's *Lohengrin* performed in Bologna.
1872	Bizet composed music for *L'Arlesienne*.
	The Bayreuth Theatre begun for the performance of operas by Wagner.
1873	Rimsky-Korsakov's *Ivan the Terrible* performed in St. Petersburg.
	Sullivan's *The Light of the World* performed at Birmingham, and César Franck's *Rédemption* in Paris.
	Debussy studied at the Paris Conservatoire.
	Verdi wrote his string quartet.
	Bruckner wrote his Second Symphony.
	Leopold Damrosch founded the Oratorio Society in New York.
1874	Queen Victoria assumed the title of Empress of India.
	Moussorgsky's *Boris Godounov* performed in St. Petersburg, and he also composed his *Pictures at an Exhibition*.
	Wagner completed his *Götterdämmerung*.
	Verdi wrote his *Manzoni Requiem*, and it was performed at St. Mark's Cathedral in Milan, and also later in the year in New York.
	Tchaikovsky composed his First Piano Concerto.
	Johann Strauss's *Die Fledermaus* performed in Vienna.
1875	Bizet's *Carmen* performed in Paris and Sullivan's *Trial by Jury* in London.
	Gounod returned to Paris. Liszt appointed head of the Hungarian Academy.
	Tchaikovsky wrote his Third Symphony.
	Hans Andersen, Danish fairy-story writer, died.
1876	The Bayreuth Theatre opened with a performance of *The Ring* cycle.
	Grieg wrote his *Peer Gynt* music.

1876 Hugo Wolf and Gustav Mahler studied at the Vienna Conservatory.
   The English Purcell Society founded.
1877 Saint-Saëns's *Samson et Dalila* performed in Weimar.
   Wagner conducted in London.
   Offenbach visited the United States.
   Borodin composed his Symphony in B minor, and visited Liszt.
1878 Gilbert and Sullivan's *H.M.S. Pinafore* performed in London.
   Beethoven's Ninth Symphony performed for the first time in Italy, at
    Milan.
   Tolstoi finished *Anna Karenina*.
1879 Bismarck concluded dual alliance with Austro-Hungarian Empire.
   Tchaikovsky's *Eugen Onegin* performed in Moscow.
   Joachim played Brahms's Violin Concerto for first time in Leipzig.
   César Franck wrote his Piano Quintet.
   Sullivan visited the United States.
1880 Tchaikovsky composed his Second Piano Concerto, Borodin com-
    posed his symphonic poem, *On the Steppes of Central Asia*, and
    Puccini studied at the Milan Conservatory.
   Bruckner wrote his Fourth Symphony.
1881 Tsar Alexander II, Emperor of Russia, is killed by a bomb.
   Sullivan's *Patience* performed in London, and Offenbach's *Tales of
    Hoffmann* in Paris.
   Charles Stanford's *The Veiled Prophet* performed in Hanover.
   R. L. Stevenson wrote *Treasure Island*.
1882 Alliance formed between Italy, Austria and Germany.
   Wagner's *Parsifal* performed at Bayreuth.
   Brahms composed his Second Piano Concerto in B♭.
   Rimsky-Korsakov wrote his opera, *The Snow Maiden*.
   Rachmaninoff studied at the St. Petersburg Conservatory.
1883 Alliance between Rumania, Austria and Germany.
   Wagner died in Venice.
   A new school of English composers arose: Mackenzie, Parry, Stanford,
    Cowen and Sullivan.
   The Royal College of Music opened in London under George Grove.
1884 Stanford's *Savonarola* performed in Hamburg, and his *Canterbury
    Pilgrims* in London.
   Massenet's *Manon* performed in Paris.
   Puccini wrote his first opera, *Le Villi*.
   Debussy won the Prix de Rome.
1885 Brahms's Fourth Symphony performed in Meiningen.
   Sullivan's *Mikado* produced in London.
   César Franck composed his *Symphonic Variations*.
   Richard Strauss succeeded von Bülow as conductor at Meiningen.
1886 Liszt died at Bayreuth.
   César Franck composed his Violin Sonata.
   Delius studied at the Leipzig Conservatory.
   Improvements made in piano construction by the firms of Blüthner,
    Bechstein and Steinway, and increased printing of music scores, etc.
1887 Verdi's *Otello* performed in Milan, and Sullivan's *Ruddigore* in London.
   Tchaikovsky toured Europe as composer-conductor.

1887	Ravel studied piano in Paris.
1888	William II, grandson of Queen Victoria, became Emperor of Germany.
	Brahms composed Double Concerto for violin and 'cello.
	César Franck composed his D minor Symphony.
	Mahler directed the Budapest Opera.
	Sullivan composed *The Yeoman of the Guard*.
	Tchaikovsky completed his Fifth Symphony.
	Richard Strauss composed his symphonic poem, *Macbeth*.
	Hugo Wolf completed *Mörike* songs and the *Eichendorf* song-cycle.
1889	Richard Strauss made Court Conductor at Weimar; he composed *Don Juan*.
	Rimsky-Korsakov and Grieg both conducted in Paris.
	Sibelius studied composition in Berlin.
	Mahler's First Symphony performed in Budapest.
	Hugo Wolf composed the *Spanisches Liederbuch* songs.
	The Eiffel Tower in Paris completed.
1890	Borodin's *Prince Igor* performed in St. Petersburg; also Tchaikovsky's *Queen of Spades*.
	Mascagni's *Cavalleria Rusticana* produced in Rome.
	Vaughan Williams studied at the Royal College of Music.
1891	Rachmaninoff wrote his First Piano Concerto.
	Dvořák composed 'Dumky' Trio, *Carneval* and *Othello* Overtures.
	Serge Prokofieff born in Russia.
1892	Brahms composed his Clarinet Quintet, fantasies and intermezzi for piano.
	Debussy completed *L'Après-midi d'un faune*.
	Dvořák went to New York as Director of the National Conservatory.
	Tchaikovsky composed *Iolanthe* and the *Nutcracker* Ballet.
	Sibelius composed *En Saga*.
	Maxim Gorky, Russian author of *My Universities*, *The Mother*, and the play *Lower Depths*, published his first story, *Mokar Chudra*.
1893	Verdi's *Falstaff* performed in Milan, and Humperdinck's *Hänsel und Gretel* in Weimar.
	Puccini's *Manon Lescaut* produced in Turin.
	Tchaikovsky died in St. Petersburg, and Gounod at St. Cloud in France.
	Dvořák wrote his 'New World' Symphony.
	Schoenberg composed Quartet in D minor.
1894	Nicholas II became Tsar of Russia.
	Mahler wrote his Second Symphony, and Bruckner his Ninth.
	George Bernard Shaw wrote *Arms and the Man*.
1895	Richard Strauss composed *Till Eulenspiegel*.
	Mahler completed his Third Symphony.
	Dvořák returned to Prague, wrote Violin Concerto in B minor and String Quartets in A♭ and G.
	Rachmaninoff wrote his First Symphony.
	Sibelius composed *The Swan of Tuonela*.
	Henry Wood directed the Queen's Hall Concerts.
	Oscar Wilde wrote *The Importance of being Earnest*.
1896	Elgar's *The Light of Life* performed at Three Choirs Festival at Gloucester Cathedral.

1896   The Schola Cantorum founded in Paris.
       Puccini's opera, *La Bohème,* performed at Turin.
       Richard Strauss composed *Also sprach Zarathustra.*
1897   Mahler appointed Artistic Director at the Vienna Opera.
       Richard Strauss completed *Don Quixote.*
       Rimsky-Korsakov's *Sadko* performed at St. Petersburg.
       Sibelius received life pension by Finnish Government in order that
          he might devote himself to composition.
       Bartók composed a piano sonata.
1898   Richard Strauss went to Berlin as conductor.
       Toscanini conducted at La Scala, Milan.
       Death of the Belgian painter, Van Gogh.
1899   The South African War began between the Boers and the British.
       Berlioz's *The Trojans,* Part I, performed in Paris.
       Elgar composed his 'Enigma' Variations.
       Schoenberg wrote his string sextet, *Verklärte Nacht.*
       Sibelius composed his First Symphony.
       Rimsky-Korsakov completed his opera, *The Tsar's Bride,* and Bartók
          composed a string quartet.
1900   Elgar's *Dream of Gerontius* performed at Birmingham, and Puccini's
          La Tosca in Rome.
       Mahler composed his Fourth Symphony.
       German and Italian musicologists published old musical works in
          modern notation, with historical commentaries.
       Rimsky-Korsakov wrote *Tsar Saltana.*
       Queen Victoria died in the Isle of Wight.
1901   Performances of: Dvořák's *Russalka* in Prague, Richard Strauss's
          Feuersnot in Dresden.
       Rachmaninoff wrote his Second Piano Concerto.
       Dvořák appointed Director of the Prague Conservatory.
1902   Debussy's opera, *Pelléas et Mélisande,* performed in Paris.
       Sibelius composed his Second Symphony and Mahler his Fifth.
       Stravinsky studied with Rimsky-Korsakov.
       The Philadelphia Orchestra formally organized.
1903   Wagner's *Parsifal* performed in New York.
       Bartók composed symphonic poem, *Kossuth,* and a violin sonata.
       John Galsworthy began his *Forsyte Saga.*
1904   The Schola Cantorum performed Monteverdi's *Orfeo* in Paris.
       Mahler composed his Sixth Symphony, and Bartók his Piano Quintet
          and Rhapsody no. 1 for orchestra.
       Prokofieff composed his First Symphony.
       Richard Strauss visited the U.S.A., and Dvořák died in Prague.
       Frequent concerts a feature of European and American society.
       Puccini's *Madame Butterfly* a failure at Milan.
       Delius's *Koanga* performed at Elberfeld.
       Anton Chekov, author of *The Cherry Orchard,* died.
1905   Unsuccessful revolution in Russia.
       Strauss's *Salome* produced in Dresden and Franz Lehar's *Merry Widow*
          in Prague.

1905 Mahler composed his Seventh Symphony, Debussy *La Mer* and
      Images for piano, Elgar *Introduction and Allegro for Strings*, and
      Bartók his First Suite for orchestra.
1906 Mozart Festival held in Salzburg.
      Wanda Landowska gave harpsichord recitals.
      Elgar visited the United States, and composed *The Kingdom*.
      Oscar Hammerstein opened the Manhattan Opera House in New York
      City.
      Ethel Smyth's *The Wreckers* performed in Leipzig.
      Henrik Ibsen, author of *Peer Gynt*, died.
1907 Delius's *Village Romeo and Juliet* performed in Berlin.
      Mahler composed his Eighth Symphony.
      Puccini and Scriabin visited America, where Richard Strauss's *Salome*
      was produced in New York.
1908 Mahler conducted in the United States and composed *Das Lied von
      der Erde*.
      Debussy's *Pelléas et Mélisande* was produced at the Manhattan Opera
      House, New York, and Toscanini conducted at the Metropolitan
      Opera House, New York.
      Vaughan Williams studied with Ravel in Paris.
      Picasso and Braque evolved cubism in art.
      Renoir painted his *Judgement of Paris*.
1909 Strauss composed *Elektra*, Vaughan Williams his *Fantasy on a Theme
      of Tallis for Strings*.
      Paderewski directed the Warsaw Conservatory.
      A Haydn Festival held in Vienna.
1910 Puccini's *Girl of the Golden West* produced in New York and Rimsky-
      Korsakov's *Golden Cockerel* in Moscow.
      Vaughan Williams wrote his 'Sea' Symphony, and Stravinsky the
      Firebird ballet.
      Elgar wrote his Violin Concerto and Debussy his *Clarinet Rhapsody*.
1911 Strauss's *Rosenkavalier* produced in Dresden.
      Stravinsky composed the ballet *Petroushka* and Ravel *Daphnis et Chloë*.
1912 Strauss composed *Ariadne auf Naxos*, Schoenberg his *Pierrot Lunaire*
      and Sibelius his Fourth Symphony.
1913 Stravinsky wrote his ballet, *Le Sacre du Printemps*, and Prokofieff his
      Second Piano Concerto.
1914 First World War.
      Vaughan Williams composed *A London Symphony*.
      Stravinsky's *Le Rossignol* produced in Paris.
1915 Strauss's 'Alpine' Symphony performed in Berlin.
      Sibelius composed his Fifth Symphony.
      Hindemith conducted opera at Frankfurt.
1916 Battles of Verdun and Somme. The Germans use gas warfare.
      Boughton's *Bethlehem* performed at Glastonbury, and Ethel Smyth's
      Bos'n's Mate and Holst's *Savitri* performed in London.
      Jazz compositions compel interest in America.
      James Joyce wrote *Portrait of the Artist as a Young Man*.
1917 Nicholas II, Tsar of Russia, abdicated in March and the October
      Revolution in Russia followed.

1917   Pfitzner's *Palestrina* performed in Munich.
        Important compositions of this year included: Debussy's Violin
        Sonata, Stravinsky's *L'Histoire du Soldat*, Prokofieff's *Classical
        Symphony* and Respighi's *Fountains of Rome*.

1918   The First World War ended with defeat of Germany.
        Bartók composed *Bluebeard's Castle* and String Quartet no. 2.
        Miaskowsky composed his Fourth and Fifth Symphonies.

1919   Treaty of Versailles.
        De Falla wrote *The Three-cornered Hat* and Elgar his 'Cello Concerto.
        Richard Strauss became Director of the Vienna Opera.

1920   League of Nations formed.
        Stravinsky composed his Symphony for Wind Instruments.
        Bloch appointed Director of the Cleveland Institute of Music.

1921   Paul Whiteman visited Europe with his jazz orchestra.
        Stravinsky composed *Mavra* and Prokofieff *The Love of Three
        Oranges*.
        Busoni's opera, *Turandot*, performed in Berlin and *King David*, a
        play with music by Honegger, in Switzerland.

1922   Vaughan Williams composed his 'Pastoral' Symphony.
        Rutland Boughton's *Immortal Hour* produced in London.
        Berg completed his opera, *Wozzeck*, based on Georg Büchner's play.
        The International Society for Contemporary Music founded and the
        first radio concert broadcast from Sheffield, England.
        Kandinsky painted *White Zigzag*.

1923   The U.S.S.R. formed.
        Compositions of note in this year included: Stravinsky's ballet, *Les
        Noces*, Schoenberg's Serenade for Seven Instruments and his
        Quintet for wind instruments, Sibelius's Sixth Symphony, Bloch's
        Baal Shem, Honegger's *Pacific 231* and Kodály's *Psalmus Hungaricus*.

1924   Compositions of this year included: Vaughan Williams's *Hugh the
        Drover*, Stravinsky's Piano Concerto.
        George Gershwin's *Rhapsody in Blue* was played at a concert of
        modern jazz at Carnegie Hall, New York.
        Sean O'Casey wrote *Juno and the Paycock*.

1925   Alban Berg's *Wozzeck* performed in Berlin, and Arnold Dolmetsch
        gave concerts of old music in England.
        Sibelius composed his Seventh Symphony, Vaughan Williams his
        Concerto Accademico and Bloch his *Concerto Grosso*.

1925   Radio requirements opened new paths for composers and musicians.

1926   General Strike in Britain in support of locked-out miners.
        Hindemith's opera, *Cardillac*, produced in Dresden and Shostakovitch
        composed his F minor Symphony.
        The first 'sound' moving picture, *Don Juan*, shown in New York,
        with music played by the New York Philharmonic Orchestra.

1927   Military control removed from Germany.
        Shostakovitch composed his 'October' Symphony.
        Weinberger's *Schwanda the Bagpiper* performed in Prague and
        Stravinsky's *Oedipus Rex* in Paris.

1927   Ernst Krenek's opera, *Johnny spielt auf* produced in Leipzig and
        Glière's *Red Poppy* ballet in Moscow.

1928   Hindemith wrote his opera, *Neues vom Tage* and Schoenberg his
        Variations for orchestra.
        Richard Strauss's opera, *The Egyptian Helen* performed in Dresden
        and Kurt Weill's *Die Dreigroschenoper* in Berlin.
        Serious musicians involved in composing for films.

1929   Bartók composed his String Quartets, nos. 3 and 4, and Shostakovitch
        his 'May' Symphony.
        Stravinsky composed Capriccio for piano and orchestra.
        Vaughan Williams's *Sir John in Love* performed in London.
        Ernest Hemingway wrote *Farewell to Arms*.

1930   Stravinsky composed his *Symphony of Psalms*.
        Copland composed his *Dance Symphony*.
        Camargo Society founded to encourage ballet in Britain.
        The Empire State Building finished in New York.

1931   William Walton's *Belshazzar's Feast* performed at Leeds.

1932   Large-scale unemployment in Britain, America and Germany.
        Compositions of this year included: Prokofieff's Piano Concerto, op. 55,
        Shostakovitch's Piano Concerto, op. 35, Rachmaninoff's Variations
        for piano on a Theme of Corelli and Ravel's Concerto for piano and
        orchestra.
        The work of Duke Ellington and other negro musicians recognized as
        a significant musical element.

1933   Hitler became Dictator of Germany.
        Richard Strauss's *Arabella* performed in Dresden.
        Schoenberg went to America.
        Bartók composed his Second Piano Concerto.

1934   Hindemith composed *Mathis der Mahler* and Stravinsky *Persephone*.

1935   Richard Strauss's *Die Schweigsame Frau* performed in Dresden.
        George Gershwin completed *Porgy and Bess*.
        T. S. Eliot wrote *Murder in the Cathedral*.

1936   Spanish Civil War.
        Richard Strauss composed *Olympic Hymn* and Rachmaninoff his
        Fourth Symphony.
        Prokofieff composed *Peter and the Wolf*.

1937   Shostakovich's fifth Symphony and Bliss's ballet *Checkmate* performed.
        Picasso painted *Guernica* expressing the horror of bombing.

1938   The German Army, under Hitler, annexed Austria.
        Benny Goodman's band dominated the Broadway scene.
        Raoul Dufy painted *Regatta* and Rouault painted *Ecce Homo*.

1939   Hitler took Czechoslovakia and invaded Poland; England and France
        declared war on Germany—the Second World War.
        Walton's Violin Concerto performed.
        James Joyce's novel *Finnegans Wake* completed.

1940   Stravinsky wrote his Symphony in C.
        Tippett's secular oratorio *A Child of Our Time* performed.
        De Mille introduced folk elements in Copland's ballet *Rodeo*.
        Brecht's play *Mother Courage* performed in U.S.A.

1941	U.S.A. declared war on Japan after attack at Pearl Harbour.
1942	The ferocity of the war almost obliterated normal living.
	U.S.S.R. became Hitler's main target and Shostakovich composed his seventh Symphony, 'Leningrad'.
1943	Vaughan Williams completed his Symphony no. 5 in D.
1944	Germany defeated by the forces of the Allies.
	Shostakovich's eighth Symphony performed.
	T. S. Eliot's *Four Quartets* published.
1945	U.S.A. dropped two atom bombs on Japan and she capitulated.
	Britten's opera *Peter Grimes* revives interest in new opera.
1946	*War and Peace* by Prokofieff performed and Shostakovich completed his ninth Symphony.
	The ballets *Symphonic Variations* by Ashton and *Fancy Free* by Robbins performed.
1947	India achieves independence.
	Walton completed his *String Quartet in A minor*.
1948	Peter Goldmark invents the long-playing record.
	Jackson Pollock shows his action painting *Composition No. 1*.
1949	Bliss's opera *The Olympians* performed.
	Britten's *Spring Symphony* performed in Amsterdam.
1950	Menotti's opera *The Consul* performed.
	'Bebop' dancing becomes fashionable.
1951	Festival of Britain brings new ideas to arts in Britain.
	Britten's *Billy Budd* and Stravinsky's *The Rake's Progress* performed.
1952	Vaughan Williams' *Romance* for harmonica and orchestra.
1953	Vaughan Williams' seventh Symphony performed.
1954	Darius Milhaud uses *musique concréte* in *La Rivière Endormie* and Shostakovich's tenth Symphony performed.
	The operas *The Turn of the Screw* by Britten and *Moses and Aaron* by Schoenberg performed.
1955	'Rock 'n Roll' dance music becomes fashionable.
1956	Stravinsky's *Canticum sacrum* performed.
1957	Francis Poulenc's opera *Dialogue des Carmelites* and Stravinsky's ballet *Agon* performed.
	Folk music revival beginning mainly as protest songs.
1958	Pizzetti's radio opera *Murder in the Cathedral* performed.
	Leonard Bernstein composed *West Side Story*.
1959	Pierre Boulez's quartet *Livre du Quattuore*, a work using advanced serial techniques, performed.
1960	Hans Werner Henze's opera *Der Prinz von Homburg* performed.
1961	Britten's opera *A Midsummer Night's Dream* performed.
	Luigi Nono's serial work *Intoleranza* performed.
1962	Tippett's opera *King Priam* in England and abroad.
1963	Britten's *War Requiem* first performed with British, Russian and German soloists.
1964	Britten's symphony with solo cello was performed by Msitslav Rostropovitch at the Aldeburgh Festival.
1965	Richard Rodney Bennett composes for children and his opera *The Mines of Sulphur* is internationally acclaimed.
	A Policy for the Arts issued; the first steps of a national plan to be implemented by the Arts Council.

CHAPTER FOURTEEN

Some General Definitions

ACOUSTICS. This means anything regarding the sense of hearing. It is used in two ways: how sound is produced and given out and what it consists of; also the suitability of a building for hearing speech or music.

Sound is caused by the vibration of something (in music a plucked string or air in a hollow tube). This sets up ripples in the air somewhat like the ripples caused by a stone being thrown into water. These ripples or waves strike the ear-drum and, provided the person or animal has hearing, set up a disturbance there which is recognized by the brain as sound.

The pitch of sound is determined by the number of vibrations per second of the body causing the sound (see EQUAL TEMPERAMENT). The loudness or intensity of sound is caused by the size of the vibrations (note that the speed of vibrations remains the same, no matter how greatly the object vibrates).

Quality of sound. A string or any other object can vibrate as a whole or in two or more separate parts and produce, not only the main note, but many other higher notes as well. These higher notes are called HARMONICS, OVERTONES or UPPER PARTIALS, and their presence in greater or lesser strength is what determines the quality or timbre of the sound produced. Harmonics can be obtained on a violin or a brass instrument by lightly touching a string in a certain place or by a certain method of blowing. In former times the only method of producing notes on a brass instrument was by producing different harmonics. When crooks or shanks were provided (see chapter on instruments of the orchestra), another note or notes were provided which could have its or their own harmonics.

Regular frequencies of vibrations give more musical notes than irregular frequencies. Therefore a rough piece of metal gives out a more unpleasant note than a smooth piece. Some vibrations, such as an organ note, can, by causing large air disturbances, shatter glass, and a loud explosion can harm the ear-drum and cause deafness.

When two loud notes are heard together, they give rise to third and fourth sounds, the differential tone and the summational tone. Tartini discovered this and, as he found that the differential is in harmony with the two notes that give rise to it, insisted that his violin students should listen to it when playing double stopping: 'If you do not hear the bass your 3rd and 6th are not in tune.'

The Transmission of Sound. Sound vibrations moving through the air are very slow compared with the speed of light. When they modulate radio waves, such as in broadcasting, which move at the speed of light, the listener at his radio set will hear music before a listener sitting at the back of a concert hall. Everyone has noticed the time-lapse between a lightning stroke and a thunder clap. This factor limits the size of forces possible for performing a work as, although everyone may see the conductor's beat simultaneously, the sound coming from the people singing at the back of a large choir may be heard by the audience at a different time from the sound coming from the violinists in the front of the orchestra.

The phenomenon of the beat or throb occurs when two notes close to each other in vibration number (see EQUAL TEMPERAMENT) are heard together. Its occurrence is due to reinforcement when the vibrations occur together, as they do at certain regular intervals. The effect can be heard when striking and holding simultaneously two of the lowest notes on the piano. It can also be heard from some types of aircraft. It is the greater or lesser intensity of these beats which forms the difference between dissonance and consonance.

Ears differ greatly in their ability to pick up extreme sounds. Some people can scarcely hear the lowest 16-ft. stop C on the organ, which vibrates at thirty-two vibrations per second. At the other end of the scale, human ears cannot hear the high sounds of the bat. They vibrate far above the 18,000 to 20,000 vibrations per second perceptible to normal ears. Sounds can be reflected from surfaces, as occurs when an echo is produced, and in round concert halls, such as the Albert Hall, London, special boards are introduced behind the platform in an attempt to 'kill' the echo.

Resonance. In scientific language, a resonator is an object made specially to respond to a specific note. In music this becomes extremely important in the design and manufacture of violins and pianos, when the shape of the bodies of the instruments makes all the difference to tone (see WOLF). It is also part of the talent of the performer to find out the best way to make the instrument he is playing resound. This, together with the 'resonance' or 'acoustics' of a hall or room, forms part of the problems a performer has to confront when playing or singing in public. (See chapter on keyboard instruments.)

ALLEMANDE. Literally 'German'. It is the name of two distinct types of composition, both of German origin. One is a dance of $\frac{4}{4}$ time in binary or two-part form. It is used by such composers as Bach, Handel, Purcell and Couperin in classical suites. The allemande still danced today by peasants of Germany and Switzerland is in $\frac{3}{4}$ time and very lively.

ARIA. This word literally means 'air'. From the eighteenth century onwards it has come to mean a lengthy and developed vocal piece in ternary or three-part form. Before then all the solo parts of opera or oratorio had almost entirely been in recitative although Monteverdi's *Arianna* (1608) contained a kind of aria. A. Scarlatti (1660-1725) developed the form further, and later composers, including Handel, produced an infinite variety of arias for every kind of occasion and performance, ranging from the *aria da chiesa* to be sung in church with an orchestral accompaniment to the difficult and elaborate *aria di bravura* (i.e. 'of boldness') such as the Queen of Night's aria in Mozart's *The Magic Flute*. Gluck, Weber, Verdi and Puccini raised the aria still further by giving it more of the meaning of the text of the opera instead of making it just a show-piece. The aria has more or less dropped out of modern opera, or music drama, as the tendency is to keep the dramatic action going, as in *Electra* and *Salome*, by

Richard Strauss. Where the old style is copied, such as in *Ariadne,* by the same composer, the aria is reinstated, as with Zerbinetta's aria. There are also arias in the operas of Benjamin Britten.

The word 'aria' is occasionally found applied to instrumental music such as occasional movements in suites of the Bach-Handel period.

ATONALITY. This is music written over the chromatic scale and is without keys. The chief exponent of this type of music is Schoenberg. (See Twelve note music).

BALLAD. Originally music both danced and sung at the same time. By the sixteenth century the word was used for Bible poetry, but the word could also be used for anything singable, if simple and for solo voice. A true ballad is a narrative poem in verse repeating form with or without refrain.

BASSO CONTINUO. This term belongs to the seventeenth and eighteenth centuries, when the harpsichordist played harmonies worked out from a figured bass and kept the music going between instrumental sections and arias.

BOURRÉE. A dance form of French origin in $\frac{4}{4}$ time like the gavotte, but with its phrases commencing on the last beat of the bar.

BRANLE. A dance type of French origin which became popular at the court of Louis XIV. It became even more popular in England. It is in $\frac{2}{4}$ time and rather like the gavotte. Branles from Poitou are in $\frac{3}{4}$ time, and it is thought that the minuet may have been derived from it.

CADENZA. A flourish before the final cadence. It began with a long trill and dates from the days of *Bel Canto* in the eighteenth century when the singer showed his ability to decorate the end of a song lavishly. The aria form of the day allowed three cadenzas. In the eighteenth century the instrumental form of Concerto took on the colour of a display piece and the performer improvised a cadenza over the themes of a concerto on the spur of the moment. In time the cadenza came to be prepared beforehand and Mozart wrote many for his pupils. Beethoven also wrote many for his concertos but very few are performed today. Nineteenth- and twentieth-century composers have usually written their own. (See Concerto).

CANON. The word means 'rule'. In music it is applied to that sort of counterpoint in which rule is most strictly followed. The rule is that the voice or instrument which begins the passage must be followed note for note by the next part which enters later. Canons can be made for two or more parts and are necessarily very difficult to write as they must always harmonize. The catch and the round are forms of canon, e.g. 'Three Blind Mice'. One of the earliest canons known is 'Sumer is icumen in', which is in six parts. This was written at the beginning of the thirteenth century. Canon occurs in the 'stretto' of a fugue. See also the chapter on form regarding variations, where an allusion is made to a canon by Beethoven. Canon is in many forms and can be accompanied by other instruments or voices. There is much imitation canon in music.

CHACONNE and PASSACAGLIA. Both originated in dances, probably coming from Spain. They are in a slow $\frac{3}{4}$ time and the music is generally built over a ground-bass.

CHORALE. Originally meant ecclesiastical plainsong. Luther took it over for the Protestant church in Germany and many chorales were written up to Bach's time.

CLASSICAL. Used in several ways: (1) that large class of music composed roughly from the end of the sixteenth century to the end of the eighteenth century, prior to the onset of the Romantic movement. (2) Music which will always be worth while hearing as against fashionable music and music which is cheap. (3) Music which is not jazz or popular music.

CONCERTO. This word originally meant several instruments playing together, and was used as far back as 1587 (the two Gabrielis). From the seventeenth century onwards it was used to describe a small body of solo strings, called 'soli' or 'concertino', played with a larger body of orchestral strings called 'ripieno'. The term 'concerto grosso' means just this, and the most famous are the six 'Brandenburg' Concertos of Bach. Since Mozart's time it has been used for one or two instruments (occasionally three) playing with orchestra. It is usually in modified three-movement sonata form with a double exposition as follows:

Exposition I	followed by Exposition II.
Orchestra alone.	Solo instrument with orchestra.
First subject in tonic often incomplete.	First subject in tonic (perhaps shortened).
Second subject, also frequently in tonic usually ending with a perfect cadence.	Second subject in dominant or relative major, usually ornamented.

The development and recapitulation are usually opened with important orchestral tuttis, which means the whole orchestra playing together. At the end of this follows the CADENZA, a florid, free fantasia on the themes of the preceding movement, originally improvised by the soloist. Nowadays traditional cadenzas are played in the old concertos, and since the days of Mendelssohn they have been written out by the composer or omitted altogether. (See Cadenza).

The other movements of the concerto are written on the lines of the movements of a sonata and are with or without cadenzas. The minuet and trio is usually not included in a concerto. The modern concerto may be called by quite different names such as 'symphonic variations', 'phantasy variations', etc.

CONCORD. For examination purposes, these are:
Concordant intervals (*concords*). All perfect intervals and all major and minor 3rds and 6ths.
Discordant intervals (*discords*). All diminished and augmented intervals and all 2nds and 7ths.

In old harmony, as explained in Example 1 in the chapter on four-part harmony, the triads are all concords except VII in major and II, III and VII in minor, the feeling being that discords should resolve into a concord. However, it must be pointed out that modern composers do not always share that view and as ears become used to serialist or twelve-note atonal music it becomes a very doubtful matter as to what is or what is not a discord.

COUNTERPOINT. Two or more melodies sounding together, which, although different from one another, usually form good harmony. (See Fugue).

COURANTE. This has existed in many rhythms and styles:

(1) The Italian type, or coranto, is in a rapid, running $\frac{3}{4}$ time.

(2) The French type, or courante. This was very popular at the Court of Louis XIV of France. It is also in $\frac{3}{4}$ time and is in simple, binary form, but with a greater variety of rhythm.

Both types were used in the old suite.

EQUAL TEMPERAMENT. Temperament means tuning an instrument so that certain gross inaccuracies between the intervals of certain notes are spread evenly over all the notes.

When a string is plucked and vibrates it gives out a sound at a certain pitch (see ACOUSTICS). A long, heavy string vibrates more slowly than a thin, short string, and the quicker the string vibrates the higher the note in pitch. Therefore, the lower notes of a piano are produced by longer and thicker strings than the higher notes. The number of vibrations can be worked out mathematically and, commencing with the lowest 16-ft. stop C on the organ, which vibrates at thirty-two vibrations per second, each succeeding C above that vibrates at exactly double the speed of the C an octave below.

As well as the note itself, the string when plucked vibrates in its other parts and produces overtones or harmonics. Thus a C gives out a faint C an octave above it and a note a 5th above that. This last note is known as a 'perfect 5th'. The plucked string also gives out fainter notes above that, with diminishing intervals between them.

In former times people usually sang in unison—that is, on the same note —or in octaves. Later on the most natural note to add was the perfect 5th and the modal melodies were accompanied by other voices singing the same melody a 5th and an octave above. This was called 'organum'. Later still it was found that the notes in between the perfect 5ths—for instance, the E between C and G or the E♭ between C and G—were the most natural notes to use in addition, and whilst the modes were still employed, this kind of harmony was quite satisfactory. When the use of the modes broke down, however, and the modern key system and modulation from one key to another gradually developed, trouble began, especially with keyboard instruments.

This was because it was found that whilst tuning in perfect octaves from C to C is very good and desirable, a rather muddled result is obtained when tuning in perfect 5ths from a C to obtain the other notes. If tuning is carried out in perfect 5ths the resulting notes are G, D, A, E, B, F♯, C♯, G♯, D♯, A♯, E♯, and B♯. This may appear to be proper and correct but B♯ will be found to be actually a quarter of a semitone above C. If all the notes are worked out correctly this means that about fifty notes are necessary within one octave. It was found impossible to devise a means to bring all these notes in an octave within the reach of the human hand quite apart from the difficulties involved of working out key modulation from such a medley of sounds. Therefore something else had to be thought out.

When the piano manufacturer started to string his instrument he found that he could tune the octaves correctly, e.g. each C string vibrating at double the speed of the C an octave below. He then had to work out an artificial number of vibrations to fit the required compass and modern key system, such as making B sharp and C the same note, and the five black notes and seven white notes of the modern keyboard were brought into being. For those who are keen on mathematics, seven semitones on our keyboard are not a perfect 5th. A perfect 5th is 7.019550008654 of a keyboard seven semitones.

Therefore, after much trial and effort, equal temperament was evolved. Bach tuned his domestic clavichords and harpsichords in this way and wrote the *Forty-eight Preludes and Fugues* in all keys, major and minor, to show the system would work, but he did not exactly invent it. The Spaniards seem to have used it two centuries before Bach, judging by the instructions in the *Musica Practica* of Ramos de Pareja, 1482, about the placing of frets on guitars, and the Italian, Zarlino, explained its application to the lute in the late sixteenth century. Elizabethan composers for the virginal have written works which employ much modulation, and therefore some sort of equal temperament must have been in use. It is therefore surprising and rather shocking that church organs in Britain were not tuned to equal temperament until the nineteenth century, and even then some organists preferred their notes 'pure' and refused to tune their instruments in any other way.

Voices and stringed instruments are still capable of performing in 'just' intonation, although most ears are probably accustomed to the sounds of equal temperament, and performers who are trained to it may not readily fall into using the perfect sounds. They have been known to do so, however, and when Joachim was accused of playing the violin out of tune some of his followers insisted that he was playing in 'just' intonation.

FIGURED BASS. This was a kind of harmonic shorthand and came into use in the seventeenth century. It was a mere line of bass notes with varying figures under or over them. The accompanist had to supply the harmony in accordance with these figures.

FUGUE. This is one of the oldest musical forms in existence. Counterpoint, or writing music in melodic lines which harmonize when overlapping, is its main feature, and it has sprung from the efforts to decorate plain themes in early music. For instance, in late medieval times it was often customary for composers to take lay music, such as folk-songs—some of quite bawdy character—and overlay them with so much counterpoint that the original theme would be completely hidden.

A fugue is developed from one good melody, called a SUBJECT, which is sung by two or more voices at different times. Look at the following well-known example from Bach's Fugue in C minor from Book I of the *Forty-eight Preludes and Fugues*:

Second voice in dominant

First voice in tonic

Counter-subject

Codetta

Free added part   etc.

Third voice in tonic

Fugues can be divided into three sections:

Enunciation or Exposition. This is given in the above example and extends to the place in the music where all the voices have entered once. The first voice usually starts in tonic, the second answers in dominant (this is called a 'real answer'), the third repeats the subject in tonic and, if there be a fourth voice, it answers again in dominant, and so on. When the theme is slightly changed in the answer it is called a Tonal Answer.

A COUNTER-SUBJECT is one which is sung against the subject. Note this and the CODETTA, which is founded on figures in the subject and counter-subject.

Modulatory Section. Here the subject and answer are given in keys other than the tonic, and are sometimes separated by a freer passage, called an 'episode'. Here is an example from the same Fugue in C minor as above:

First middle entry of subject in key of E♭

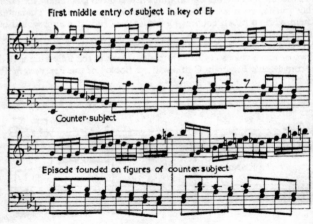

Counter-subject

Episode founded on figures of counter-subject

Second middle entry
in key of C minor

Final Section. This section is usually marked by the entrance of the subject and answer in tonic. Sometimes it includes a passage in stretto, which in this sense means that the voices are written overlapping each other or nearer together. The following is an example, also from Book I of the *Forty-eight Preludes and Fugues* by Bach, and is in B♭ minor:

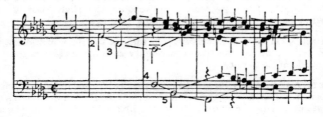

Lines indicate the entry of each of the five voices.

The coda to a fugue begins after the end of the last entry or subject and answer in the tonic key. Sometimes, as in the aforementioned Fugue in C minor, it begins on a tonic pedal. See the example by Bach on page 50.

GAVOTTE. A French dance which became popular at the Court of Louis XIV. It is in $\frac{4}{4}$ time and simple binary form. It became one of the optional movements of the classical suite.

GIGUE. This was originally an English, Scottish or Irish folk-dance type. It was first mentioned in literature by John Garland in 1230. English composers first used it for works for virginal and lute in the late sixteenth century, and it appeared on the Continent for the first time in 1649 in works by Froberger.

As the suite developed, it usually became the dance used to end the cycle.

It is a dance of $\frac{3}{4}$ time or a multiple of 3—3, 6, 9 or 12—and is in simple binary form.

GROUND OR GROUND-BASS. A very early variant of variation form, it consists of a short piece of bass repeated over and over again with varied upper parts. It is used in 'Sumer is icumen in', written in the early part of the thirteenth century (Canon), Purcell's song, 'When I am laid in earth' from the opera, *Dido and Aeneas*, the last movement of Brahms's Fourth Symphony, the finale of his *Variations on a Theme of Haydn* and Elgar's *Carillon*.

INVENTION. The name given by Bach to two and three-part compositions for the keyboard, written that pupils might 'learn to acquire good ideas . . . to work them out themselves . . . and at the same time to gain a strong predeliction for composition'.

KÖCHEL. Ludwig von (1800-1877) catalogued and numbered the works of Mozart, who had not used opus numbers, in chronological order as K.1 to K.500., etc.

MASQUE OR MASK. An elaborate type of entertainment in vogue in England during the reigns of James I and Charles I and usually based upon mythology. It combined a poetic text, vocal and instrumental music with dancing and colourful costumes, decorations and scenery. The famous masque *Comus*, by John Milton, was given in 1634 at Ludlow Castle and included music by Lawes, Campian, Locke and Gibbons, etc.

MASS. The celebration of the Eucharist or Lord's Supper in the Roman Catholic Church. The Low Mass is spoken, but the High Mass has music included in six sections, some of them subdivided again.

METRICAL PSALTER. A paraphrasing in verse of the Book of Psalms, which became popular during the sixteenth century as congregations began to join in the music of the service.

MINUET. A slow, stately French dance, generally believed to have originated in the province of Poitou. The name is derived from the French word *menu*, meaning small, describing the rather short steps employed in the dance. The simple triple tempo was always quite moderate. It was, like so many other dance forms, often incorporated in the instrumental suites and partitas of composers like Handel, Bach, Mozart and others.

MODES. See page 18.

MORRIS DANCE. An old English folk dance, possibly evolved from the sword dance known in the fifteenth century, or from a Moorish dance called the Morisco. Commonly incorporated in pageants concerning Robin Hood during May celebrations. Tunes used for this dance are still preserved and are in duple, triple and quadruple time.

NEO-CLASSICAL. In the style of classical music, but composed by a modern musician, e.g.—the Classical Symphony by the Russian Prokofieff written in 1917 and intended by him to be a modern version of Mozart.

OPUS. (Abbreviated Op.). The Latin word for work, used for the first time by seventeenth-century composers in numbering their compositions. The opus number may or may not indicate the date of composition. Some composers number their works as they are completed, while others number them according to the date of publication. A single opus may be long, as for example Beethoven's first Six Quartets which comprise his Opus 18. Nos. 1, 2, 3, 4, 5, and 6 or it may be a single short piece.

ORATORIO. A large-scale dramatic composition usually based upon a sacred text, presented in a church or concert hall by soloists, choir and orchestra without costume or action.

OVERTURE. Usually an orchestral piece preceding an opera or oratorio. Its form has varied over the years, but first reached some kind of definite framework with the French overtures of Lully and the Italian overtures of Alessandro Scarlatti, both conceived at about the same time. They had no connection with the following drama, and when detached and played separately at concerts they provided the seed of the symphony.

Gluck was the first composer to ally his overture to the drama, and since then most overtures present in musical terms some of the material of the following opera or oratorio.

Most nineteenth-century overtures are in first movement sonata form.

PASSACAGLIA. An old Italian or Spanish dance of stately character which became very popular as a form for instrumental composition in the seventeenth and eighteenth centuries. It is constructed on a ground-bass like a chaconne.

PASSEPIED. First danced in the streets of Paris in 1578 and originated by Breton sailors, it was later introduced into the ballet. It is in $\frac{3}{4}$ time and a little quicker than a minuet. There are two or more repeated sections using the major and minor key. It was also used as part of instrumental suites.

PAVAN and GALLIARD. The association of two dance types is very common in the instrumental music of the late sixteenth century and marks the beginning of the suite.

The *pavan* came from Padua in Italy, is in a slow and majestic $\frac{2}{4}$ time, and was therefore used in processions. It became popular in Spain. Modern composers are still using this form. Examples are *Pavane pour une Infante défunte* (*Pavan for a Dead Infanta*) and Pavan in the *Mother Goose Suite*, both by Ravel. Vaughan Williams has also written 'Pavan of the Heavenly Host' and 'Galliard of the Sons of Morning' in his ballet, *Job*.

The *galliard* is in striking contrast to the *pavan*, and is in a quick $\frac{3}{4}$ time. Also Italian in origin, it became very popular in Elizabethan England. It has five steps fitted to six beats, the last beat having no step.

The Pavan and Galliard lost their popularity as dances in the seventeenth century to the saraband and the gigue.

PEDAL. Part of the mechanism of the organ, piano and harp. On the organ three different arrangements of pedals are used: (1) for bass notes, (2) for governing the swell box, and (3) for altering registration. On the piano the left pedal (indicated on the score as una corda (*q.v.*)) softens the tone by a mechanical change of the action and the right pedal adjusts the dampers in a way which causes the strings to vibrate more freely, thus sustaining the tone longer than otherwise (see chapter on signs). A few pianos still have a centre pedal which can have different functions, but usually it is to make a treble melody more prominent and muffle the accompanying bass or to hold any note (or sustain it) whilst a passage is being played staccato elsewhere on the piano keyboard.

On the harp the pedals shift the pitch of the strings up a semitone, or a tone, at the will of the player. (See Chapter 10).

PITCH. Another instance of how scientific invention and artistic expression have moved hand in hand all through history. Pythagoras, a Greek mathematician and philosopher of about 500 B.C. invented a system for measuring pitch which established definite vibrations per second for any given note within his two-octave scale. This eventually enabled instruments to be tuned exactly as required and not indefinitely. Composers were then able to gauge the effect of their compositions and know that when played and sung as written they would follow exactly the height or depth of pitch that had been planned. Unfortunately, various countries could not come to an agreement, and for many hundreds of years no standard pitch obtained, and this gave rise to a good deal of confusion when the musicians of different countries met to play or sing together. However, in 1939 an international pitch was at last agreed and the A above middle C was fixed at 440 vibrations per second and all other notes could be measured and adjusted from that. (See Chapter 10).

PLAINSONG. A style of church music used before the rise of polyphony. For a long time it had no time divisions and was often taught orally. All early unmeasured music should be called 'plainsong', but the Gregorian collection of Latin plainsong has become so famous in history that most people concentrate on that alone when studying plainsong.

POLYPHONY. The combining of two or more lines of melody, which dates from the use of organum (or double melody). This emphasis on combining melodies, rather than considering harmony and the progression of chords as of equal importance, changed gradually until in the sixteenth century and onwards they became of parallel concern. (See Fugue).

RECITATIVE. The part of opera or oratorio which usually links the arias and choruses, and is a declamation by a solo singer of a dramatic action or thought. The older form was called *recitativo secco*, in which simple chords accompanied a quickly-moving patter of words either spoken or sung, accentuating the natural stresses of the language.

Later, this developed into *recitativo stromentato*, which was set to a fully composed orchestral background.

RHAPSODY. A title for a musical composition of a high-spirited and dramatic nature first by Liszt. Its origin is Greek and was the name of a professional reciter of epic ballads.

ROMANTIC. As applied to music is supposed to describe the compositions of such musicians as Brahms, Chopin, Schumann, Tschaikovsky, Liszt, Schubert, Mendelssohn and others composing roughly from 1825 to 1850. Music which portrays personal emotion, often with literary associations, popularly comes under this heading, but it is a loose term.

SARABAND. A stately dance of obscure origin, but well known in England, France and Spain at the beginning of the sixteenth century. It is in simple triple time and a strong accent falls on the second beat in each bar.

SHANTY. Old worksongs sung by sailors of the eighteenth and nineteenth centuries. The leader of the singing was called the shanty man.

SICILIANA. This was originally a dance song from Sicily, but was used later by composers as a movement in suites, preserving in it a special rhythm in compound duple time.

SUITE or **PARTITA**. A collection of pieces, orchestral or for keyboard instruments, based on popular dances of the sixteenth and seventeenth centuries. These tunes and rhythms were known in all musically advanced countries and were freely interchanged by musicians travelling in Europe. The order and choice of the dances, such as pavan, galliard, almanes (or allemande) and branles in the late sixteenth century were not fixed except by the taste of the individual composer, who drew contrasted moods and times from all countries, or by the fashionable wishes of the dancers.

Towards the close of the seventeenth century the suite became an orchestral or keyboard work of rather formal design, not necessarily used for actual dancing, but played at concerts. There was a more limited choice of dances and a more or less prescribed order was expected, the most common of which was allemande, courante, sarabande and gigue. The only really definite rule was the use of one key only for the complete suite, and there were very few exceptions.

A popular modern example is the *Capriol Suite* by Peter Warlock, although this does not adhere to one key.

SYMPHONIC POEM was a title invented by Liszt to describe a large orchestral work not based rigidly on the symphonic form, but having a freer range of musical expression allied more closely to a poetic or dramatic programme. Composers in many countries eagerly began to compose in this new style, and some of the works written were *Ma Vlast*, by Smetana, *Steppes of Central Asia*, by Borodin, *Romeo and Juliet*, by Tchaikovsky, *Don Juan*, by Richard Strauss, and in more modern times *Fountains of Rome*, by Resphighi and *La Mer*, by Debussy.

SYMPHONY now means an extended full orchestral work, with usually three or four contrasted movements. But the term was first used in the early part of the seventeenth century to describe any short orchestral interlude in a cantata or choral piece, where the main interest really lay in the vocal parts. It was also loosely applied to introductions to a vocal solo, even when played on a keyboard instrument.

Later, in the seventeenth century, the overture (*q.v.*) of operas, especially French ones by composers such as Lully, began to acquire a form which in turn developed into what was called the 'Italian overture', and this was the real seed of the modern symphony. It was divided into three movements, the first and last quick and the middle one slow. By the 1750s this had become an accepted musical convention, and Mozart used it in his early opera *La finta semplice* (K.51). However, the general attention of audiences was not concentrated on the entertainment until the dramatic part of the opera began so these symphonies tended to be composed without relation to the drama which followed and very soon began to be detached and used as orchestral pieces at concerts (see chapter on musical form).

TETRACHORD. See page 19.

TONIC SOL-FA. A method of musical notation for teaching and especially useful in establishing a facility for sight reading vocal music. It is best suited for the study of music composed in the conventional major and minor keys in which there is infrequent modulation from one key to another. It cannot be applied to music composed in any of the twelve note scale systems.

TROUBADOUR. Poet musicians of the nobility of southern France who played and sang towards the close of the eleventh century and onwards for about two further centuries. Their talent was encouraged by Eleanor of Aquitaine, who, on her marriage to the French King Louis VII, carried her enthusiasm with her to the northern provinces and there established the

TROUVÈRE, poet musicians of northern France. Many examples of lyrics and melodies performed by these musicians have survived and are obtainable for study. They are important in the history of music, as they fixed the form of some later songs and dances.

TUNING FORK. A reliable instrument for supplying an exact pitch, invented in 1711 by John Shore, a famous trumpeter who played for Handel.

TWELVE–NOTE MUSIC (from the German word, *Zwölftonmusik*). A name given to several series of twelve-note groupings taken from the chromatic scale and used as a basis for composition instead of the more usual major and minor forms. The composer, Schoenberg, and his pupils, Berg and Webern, composed with this technique, and some later musicians have written works in a similar idiom.

UNA CORDA (one string). These words on a piano score indicate the use of the left pedal. When depressed on old grand pianos, the action was shifted slightly to one side and resulted in the hammers striking only one string instead of three. On modern pianos two strings are struck. In upright pianos the usual change in mechanism alters the distance between the hammers and the string, making the blow a shorter and less-powerful one. In all cases it produces a soft, shimmering tone.

WAITS. Originally night guards at the city gates, and they were provided with a reed instrument for giving signals or sounding 'All's well'. By the fifteenth and sixteenth centuries they had developed into official bands employed by the towns and cities for civic functions. They were, in effect, the first municipally supported musicians. In due course they produced distinguished players such as the father of Orlando Gibbons and of John Banister.

WOLF. A term applied to a fault in a stringed instrument, which produces a rough, jarring sound on a particular note. It is usually impossible to remedy, and when acquiring a new and possibly expensive instrument the purchaser should check carefully the tone of each string.

Bibliography

HISTORY

Man and His Music. Harman and Mellers. (Barrie & Rockliff.)
The Music Masters. Bacharach. (Pelican.)
Oxford History of Music. Ed. Wellesz. (O.U.P.)
The Pelican History of Music. Ed. Stevens and Robertson. (Pelican.)
Some Great Composers. Eric Blom. (O.U.P.)
Master Musician Series. Eric Blom. (Dent.)
Music—A Short History. Evelyn Porter. (Hutchinson.)
Source Readings in Music History. Oliver Strunk. (Faber.)
Historical Chronology of Music, with questions. Holmes and Kahn. (A. Weeks.)
The Growth of Music. Colles. (O.U.P.)
Twentieth-Century Music. (Pelican.)
Recorded History of Music in Sound. Recording. (HLP 1-27.)

INSTRUMENTS

Musical Instruments Through the Ages. Baines. (Pelican.)
Musical Instruments. Geiringer. (Allen & Unwin.)

COMPOSITION, ANALYSIS, PERFORMANCE

Melody Writing and Analysis. A. O. Warburton. (Longmans.)
Harmony. A. O. Warburton. (Longmans.)
First Year Harmony. Lovelock. (Hammond.)
Harmony and Musical Effect. Paul Davis. (Barrie & Rockliff.)
Form in Music. Stewart Macpherson. (Joseph Williams.)
Musical Forms and Textures. N. Demuth. (Barrie & Rockliff.)
Form in Brief. Lovelock. (Bell.)
The Symphony. Ralph Hill. (Pelican.)
The Concerto. Ralph Hill. (Pelican.)
Chamber Music. A. Robertson. (Pelican.)
Guide to Orchestral Music. Frank Howes. (Collins.)
Concert Goers Library of Descriptive Notes. Rosa Newmarch. (O.U.P.)
Complete Book of Opera. Gustav Kobbe. (Putnam.)
An Introduction to the Performance of Bach. Roselyn Tureck. 3 Vols. (O.U.P.)
The Interpretation of Early Music. Robert Donington. (Faber.)
What is Jazz? A recorded lecture by Leonard Bernstein. (Philips BBL 7149.)

GENERAL

Grove's Dictionary of Music and Musicians. Several vols. (Macmillan.)
Oxford Companion to Music. Blom. (O.U.P.)
A New Dictionary of Music. Arthur Jacobs. (Pelican.)
Music Encyclopedia. Westrup and Harrison. (Collins.)
The Student's Pronouncing and Musical Dictionary. L. Aubry. (Lengnick.)

Index